Behind the Screen

with Ubuntu and LibreOffice

by Steve Hayes

Any sufficiently advanced technology is indistinguishable from magic. *Arthur C. Clarke*

First Edition, May 2012

Copyright © 2011-2012 by Stephen J Hayes

ISBN 978-1-4717-1731-4

TRADEMARKS/REGISTERED TRADEMARKS
Computer hardware and software brand names mentioned in this book are protected by their respective trademarks and are acknowledged here.

To my wife, partner and best friend Lynne
whose helplessness before the infernal machine
inspired this book

Table of Contents

Preface

- Are you just starting out with a computer that you'll use to write letters, reports and other documents? Maybe you haven't even bought the computer yet.

- Have you been using a computer with a word processor and perhaps a spreadsheet for some time but still find it intimidating and feel that you don't understand what it's doing?

If you fit either description and want to use Ubuntu, this book is meant for you. It isn't intended for experienced power-users of a word processor or spreadsheet although they may pick up some useful ideas.

Why this book?

If you've browsed in a bookshop, you'll have seen many vast tomes covering word processors and spreadsheets. This book aims to be different:

- It's much shorter, covering stuff you'll actually use.

- It covers free open-source programs instead of expensive proprietary ones.

- It covers basic skills you need to use your computer as well as how to use the word processor and spreadsheet.

- It leads you through a voyage of discovery: you learn by seeing what needs to be done and then doing it.

- It explains concepts and jargon and tries to give you a mental image of how things work. You'll remember how to do them, see how to do similar tasks and be better placed to figure it out when something you try to do goes wrong.

- It doesn't pretend that things always go as they should.

- Although it specifically covers LibreOffice, it tries to be general enough so that you can use other word processors and spread-sheets too.

Because it's very easy to become stymied and dispirited due to a trivial misunderstanding, each chapter works through an exercise step-by-step and early chapters do this in detail with many screenshots. Later chapters assume familiarity with basic operations such as finding something in a dialogue box.

Often there's a choice between doing something the fastest and most efficient way and doing it in a way that's easier to understand and remember. Except for things you'll do often, this book favours the way that's easier to remember.

The exercises are chosen to be as quick and easy as possible to follow while still illustrating concepts, pitfalls and the capabilities of LibreOffice. Once you're familiar with LibreOffice, you'll make documents that are much nicer than the ones produced here.

What operating system?

Microsoft Windows is the most widely known operating system.

> *There are other versions of this book covering Microsoft Office or LibreOffice installed on Windows.*

You've decided to be more adventurous and use LibreOffice and Ubuntu in place of Microsoft Office and Windows. You can expect a few frustrations but, once you're familiar with Ubuntu, you'll hate it when you have to use Windows with its sluggishness, its security problems, its glut of unwanted software (crapware) and its expensive applications.

> *Linux is an open-source version of the very powerful Unix operating system. Ubuntu is the best known Linux distribution but there are many others including Fedora and Mint. Ubuntu recently introduced their new Unity interface which starts programs using the Launcher in place of start menus.*
>
> *Some people who were used to the old menus have switched to Mint making it the most popular distribution at the time of writing. As a new user, you're more likely to enjoy Unity which offers a route forward into the era of tablet computing.*

What word processor?

The book covers use of the open-source LibreOffice Writer word processor which is automatically included in your Ubuntu installation.

> *This book was written and formatted using Ubuntu and LibreOffice.*

You might have considered using Microsoft Word instead, even though it costs real money and, for most users, has few additional features. There are two main reasons you might prefer Word:

- It's widely used by businesses and knowing how to use it effectively can be an advantage in the job market.

- Although LibreOffice can save documents in the file format used by Word, there can be minor glitches when these files are opened in Word.

Word is part of Microsoft Office. Less expensive versions of Office may not be licensed for commercial use, even in a small or home business. LibreOffice has no such restrictions.

You can use an emulator such as wine to run Microsoft Office in Ubuntu but it's complex and could be troublesome. If you want to use Word, you should probably stick to Windows.

What spreadsheet?

LibreOffice includes the Calc spreadsheet as well as the Writer word processor.

The best known and most widely used spreadsheet is Microsoft Excel (also part of Microsoft Office). Much of what's covered here applies to Excel too.

1 Introduction

1.1 Taking it in

It would be nice if a computer was something like a toaster and a four page instruction leaflet was all that was needed. Unfortunately it isn't like that...

It's not a good idea to read this book all the way through and try to learn everything in each chapter as you go along. You'll get overwhelmed. It's better to work through the exercises, just remembering the bits that seem immediately useful. After you start using them, skim through the chapters again. More of the details will seem relevant.

Perhaps do one chapter a day. You'll remember things better once you've slept on them.

Chapter 2 shows how your computer works and explains a lot of jargon. Chapter 3 helps you to install Ubuntu. Chapters 4, 6 and 12 show how to use Ubuntu itself.

Chapter 5 covers the basics of word processing. The concepts and capabilities it describes apply to most word processors, including Microsoft Word.

Chapter 7 covers useful features that even many experienced word processor users seem unaware of. Chapters 8 and 9 cover spreadsheets.

Chapters 10, 11 and 13 cover more advanced word processing: chapter 10 mentions the LibreOffice Math formula editor and chapter 11 touches on the LibreOffice Draw program. You can skim these very quickly just to see what's there, then work through their exercises once you know that the material covered will be useful. If all you want to do is to write the occasional letter, this may be never.

LibreOffice includes Impress (similar to Microsoft Powerpoint) and the Base database program. This book doesn't cover those at all.

There is a comprehensive index.

1.2 Conventions

When an important term is introduced, it's shown in **bold**.

From Chapter 3 on, you'll be following through exercises on your computer. In some cases, you need to type in a specific phrase or look for a phrase in a dialogue box or drop-down menu. These are shown in italics, e.g. type *The quick brown fox jumps over the lazy dog.*

There are optional paragraphs formatted in italics like this one. They contain information that may be interesting, useful and helps you to understand the steps being described. You can safely skip over them if you want to. Come back and read them later.

The steps are divided into sections. Each section introduces a few concepts. There's a list of these concepts at the end of the section entitled *What you learned.* Don't worry if you didn't learn all of them – just come back later.

Some of these concepts were only covered in the optional paragraphs. They're shown in italics too. If you skipped the optional paragraphs, you shouldn't worry about these concepts.

2 Behind the screen

The magical and powerful Wizard of Oz turned out to be someone very ordinary standing behind a curtain. Computers may be powerful but they ain't magical.

"I'm thinking of buying a computer. It has:

- **An Intel Dual Core 3.3GHz processor**

- **4GB of RAM**

- **A 500GB hard drive**

- **An Intel HD2000 Graphics adapter**

- **Windows 7"**

Sounds impressive but what does it all mean? Once you've read this chapter, you'll know. You'll also find it easier to understand why your computer behaves the way that it does.

Let's start with a machine from the age before computers.

Photo author: Dominic Alves, Brighton, England

This is a teleprinter machine. Like a typewriter, it has a keyboard and a printing mechanism but it can be connected to another similar machine, perhaps thousands of miles away. When the operator presses a key on the keyboard, the corresponding letter is printed on the distant machine. Before these machines were introduced, messages had to be sent by skilled operators using Morse code – teleprinters made things much easier.

On the left hand side of the machine are a roll of **paper tape** and mechanisms to punch and read it. We'll have a closer look at these because a modern computer uses an electronic equivalent of paper tape to store what you type into it.

When the paper tape punch is switched on and the operator presses a key, a row of holes is punched in the tape and it moves forward one row. A whole message can be saved on tape and stored. At any time, it can be fed back through the reader and the message printed out or sent to a distant teleprinter.

Paper Tape

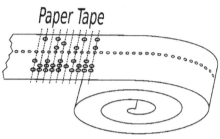

Here's a length of tape with the words *Paper Tape* punched into it. Each letter corresponds to a row of holes in the tape – a coded letter (though not a secret code). The letters *a*, *p* and *e* occur twice and the pattern of holes is the same both times. Also notice that a row was punched when the operator pressed the spacebar between the two words. When the tape is fed through the reader, this row doesn't print anything but, just like when the spacebar is pressed, it causes the printing position to move forward, leaving a blank space.

> *The tape, when bought new, already has the small holes. Each row that is punched can contain up to eight of the larger holes, three on the far side of the small hole and five on the near side. (It happens that the words Paper Tape don't cause any holes to be punched in the nearest position on the tape or in the position just this side of the small holes.)*

You could think about doing some clever things with paper tape.

- You could print the same message many times.
- You could make copies of the tape (the teleprinter itself can do this).
- You could post a copy to someone.
- You could cut up the tape and stick the pieces together to rearrange the words, sentences, etc.

These, of course, are things you can do with a word processor. It does

2 Behind the screen

them in much the same way as you could with paper tape, scissors and glue, even using the same codes for the keys pressed, but it does them much more quickly and easily because it keeps the codes in an electronic memory.

2.1 Bits, bytes, characters, numbers and data

At each row on the paper tape, you saw that there can be up to 8 holes. There are 256 (2^8) possible patterns of holes that could be punched in each row (including no holes at all).

Each place that a hole could be represents one binary digit or **bit** of data. If a hole is present, we say it's a binary 1. If it's absent, we say it's a binary zero.

Instead of the presence or absence of a hole, a bit can be represented by an electrical voltage or current – one value represents a zero, a different value represents a 1.

We refer to 8 bits as a **byte** and, as noted above, a byte can have any of 256 possible values. A selection of these can be used to represent various **characters** – the 26 capital letters (*A-Z*), the 26 lower case ones (*a-z*), the digits *0-9*, the various punctuation symbols, space and other functions such as RETURN (new line). The commonest selection is the ASCII (*American Standards Committee for Information Interchange*) code used by the teleprinter machine above.

Or a byte can represent a number in the range 0 to 255 (or perhaps -128 to +127). Two bytes taken together (16 bits) can represent numbers in the range 0 to 65,535 (0 to 2^{16}-1). Four bytes (32 bits) can represent numbers in the range 0 to 4,294,967,295.

> *Binary numbers of various lengths can be written out (should you ever need to) as a series of ones and zeroes but, if they are long, that quickly gets confusing. It's common to put the bits in groups of four (giving 16 possible values) and represent each group as a number 0-9 or letter A-F. This is hexadecimal notation.*

The term **data** just means information that is stored or transmitted.

2.2 Kilo, Mega, Giga and Tera

In conventional language, **kilo** is 1000, **mega** is 1 million, **giga** is 1000 million (usually called a billion) and **tera** is a million million (1000 billion). For example, a kilometre is 1000 metres.

In some situations with computers (which are pointed out later), different values are used. Kilo can be 2^{10} (1,024), mega can be 2^{20} (1,048,576) and giga can be 2^{30} (1,073,741,824).

2.3 The computer

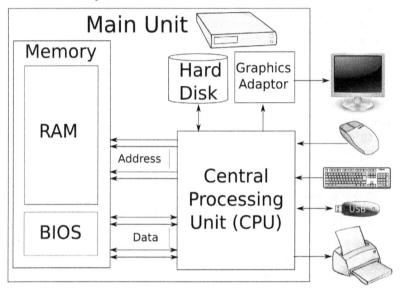

As this diagram shows, the main unit of a typical desktop computer contains (among other things) memory devices, a CPU, a hard disk drive (perhaps more than one) and a graphics adaptor. The memory and CPU are plugged into a large printed circuit board (the **motherboard**). The graphics adaptor may be part of the motherboard or it may be a separate plug-in card.

A display screen (monitor), mouse and keyboard are connected to the main unit. With a laptop, the screen and keyboard are built into the main unit along with, usually, a touchpad in place of the mouse.

The **CPU (Central Processing Unit)** is the heart of the computer. It's a microchip containing complex electronic logic circuits, usually made by Intel (e.g. Pentium) or AMD (e.g. Athlon).

The **memory** is like a huge array of pigeon-holes, each able to hold one byte of data (making each one equivalent to a row on a paper tape). A number is sent from the CPU to the memory over the address bus to select a particular pigeon-hole. The address bus might consist of 32 separate electrical paths on the motherboard – these could select any of 4,294,967,296 pigeon-holes although they may not all exist.

Because of the way the addresses work, computer memories have a size which is a power of two. For this reason, their sizes are quoted using the alternative definitions of kilo, mega and giga mentioned previously. For example, a 1 GB (gigabyte) memory can store 1,073,741,824 bytes.

When the CPU needs to store or retrieve a byte, it uses the address bus to select the required location (pigeon-hole). If it's storing a byte there, it drives the data bus (consisting of eight separate electrical paths) to the voltages representing the byte it wants to store. If it's retrieving a byte, the memory drives the data bus and the CPU looks at the voltages to see what is stored in that pigeon-hole.

There's some simplification here. To speed things up, modern computers have 32 or 64 paths in the data bus and can access 4 or 8 successive bytes at the same time.

2.4 Programs and Data

As you saw, bytes stored in the memory can represent characters or numbers, but they can also represent instructions for the CPU. When the computer first starts up, the CPU reads successive bytes from the memory starting at a fixed location and performs the operations that they specify. For example, an instruction might say to add numbers from two different locations in memory and store the result in a third location. Another instruction might say to compare characters from two locations in memory and, if they match, start fetching instructions from a different location instead of the usual next one.

Although each instruction only specifies a simple operation, a long sequence of them can do something apparently very complex and sophisticated. A modern computer can carry out billions of instructions every second.

A sequence of instructions makes up a program. Your word processor is a program with millions of instructions. Some of them need to be carried out many times over to accomplish even an apparently trivial task such as showing a letter on the screen.

We'll refer to instructions for the CPU stored in the memory as **Programs** and everything else (for example, word-processor documents) as **Data**.

When the CPU is following instructions for a program, we say that the program is **running** or **executing** (they mean the same thing).

2.5 Bugs

When a program contains millions of instructions, it inevitably has some logic errors. An error in a program is often referred to as a **bug**. Major bugs are spotted and fixed quite quickly but ones that are only seen intermittently or under unusual circumstances can persist for years before a programmer tracks down what's causing the problem and fixes it.

> *The expression originated when an early computer malfunctioned because of a moth trapped in one of its relays.*

2.6 Crashes and viruses

You're probably wondering how the CPU knows which parts of the memory contain programs and which contain data. The answer is that, in general, it doesn't know. Programs are designed so that, after the CPU processes each instruction, it gets another instruction, not some other piece of data.

Sometimes this goes wrong and the CPU starts treating data as instructions. This rarely causes anything interesting to happen. Sometimes the computer just freezes up. Other times, it detects that there's a problem and either stops the faulty program or stops entirely with an error message (a **crash**). The message may include long numbers in the hexadecimal notation described earlier – only the programmer can make sense of these.

Because of flaws in some of the programs on the computer, malicious people can use various tricks to get it to start running a program that shouldn't be there. This is a computer virus.

> *Strictly speaking, the correct term for all malicious programs is **malware**. A virus is malware of a particular type.*
>
> *An attack often starts when your computer opens something on a page of a dubious website or something attached to a spam e-mail.*
>
> *Once an attacker has got one malware program onto a computer, they can use it to install more programs whenever they like. It's common for them to install a program that uses*

your computer and internet connection to send vast numbers of spam e-mails. They can also use it and thousands like it to overload commercial websites, holding them to ransom.

*A **keylogger** is a very nasty form of malware. It records every key that you press and sends the information over the internet to an attacker. For example, they can see your passwords. That's why most banks require you to click things on the screen to log in – it's much harder to capture that.*

*Attackers mainly target Windows systems: Linux systems such as Ubuntu have historically been less vulnerable. Windows has improved and is now about equally secure but, because it is much more common, it's still a more tempting target. Many different **anti-virus** programs are available for Windows.*

At the time of writing, the malware threat to Ubuntu systems is too low to make it worthwhile installing an anti-virus program. You should still keep your password secure, keep your system up to date (see Section 12.8), avoid installing anything from a dubious source and keep a lookout for news reports in case a threat emerges. If so, a program such as *clamav* can be installed (see Section 12.1).

2.7 RAM and Hard Disks

Most of the memory in the computer is RAM. This stands for Random Access Memory – the name goes back to the earliest computers and isn't particularly meaningful for us. What's significant is that data stored in RAM is lost when the computer shuts down. Copies of programs and important data such as your word-processed documents need to be kept on the hard disk. Some people think of the disk as being part of the computer's memory but we'll view it as something separate.

The hard disk contains a number of spinning disks which have a coating similar to that used on recording tapes. Magnetic heads can record data as a series of magnetised regions on the coating, then play them back and recover the data. The magnetised data remains when power is off and the disk can hold much more data than would fit into an affordable amount of RAM. However, the CPU needs to use a program to write data to and fetch it from the hard disk and this is perhaps a million times slower than saving it in and getting it from RAM.

Because the disk is not addressed in the same way as the RAM, 1GB of hard disk space usually means 1,000,000,000 bytes (the conventional meaning of giga) rather than the 1,073,741,824 bytes that 1 GB of RAM could hold.

2.8 The BIOS and booting

Now here's a puzzle. If the CPU needs a special program to get data from the disk and any program in RAM is lost when the computer is shut down, how can it start up again? The answer is the **BIOS** memory. This is a different type of memory known as ROM (Read Only Memory). Data in the ROM is loaded at the factory and is permanent (often a Flash memory is used instead which you can reprogram but that's a complex and risky process). When the computer starts, the CPU begins fetching instructions at a fixed location in the BIOS memory where there's a program that can access the hard disk, copy further programs from it into the RAM and start them. This is the **boot** process – a term inspired by the image of the computer lifting itself by its own bootstraps.

The BIOS allows various options to be set when the computer starts up – you need to hold down a particular key or combination of keys when the computer starts to get to the options. For example, the BIOS can be set to load a program from a DVD or thumbdrive instead of the hard disk when the computer starts. This is the way that programs such as the operating system are installed on (copied to) a new computer.

2.9 Writing a program

This is far beyond the scope of this book but a quick overview might be interesting.

A program as stored on the hard disk or in RAM may make sense to the CPU but it makes no sense to you or me – it's just a series of meaningless bytes.

Programs are written in a more user-friendly language using a program quite like a word-processor. The new program (known as **source code**) is translated to instructions understood by the CPU using another program known as a compiler.

Examples of programming languages are Basic, C, C++, C#, Cobol, Fortran, Java, Perl and Python. There are many more, rather more than we really need.

2.10 Operating Systems and Applications

The **operating system** consists of the program that's loaded from the hard disk and started by the BIOS plus a large collection of additional programs that can be started and used to do basic computing tasks such as maintaining data on the hard disk. We'll see some of these programs later on. Examples of operating systems are the various versions of Microsoft Windows, Apple's OS-X and open-source Linux systems such as Ubuntu.

> *Open-source means that the source code of the program is published freely and anyone who wants to can improve it. Open-source programs, including LibreOffice, OpenOffice and versions of Linux including Ubuntu are normally available at no cost.*

Applications (or **apps**) are programs which aren't part of the operating system itself although sometimes they may be included with it. Most Linux versions (including Ubuntu) include LibreOffice or OpenOffice as a word processor and spreadsheet.

Windows includes a very basic word processor – WordPad. The best known word processor, Microsoft Word, is an application not included in Windows itself – it must be paid for and installed separately.

> *Smartphones are also little computers with an operating system (e.g. Android – derived from Linux) and apps.*

2.11 The keyboard, mouse and display

Programs running on the CPU need to be able to tell which keys are pressed on the keyboard and when and where the mouse is moved. We don't need to examine how this is done.

Programs also need to control the display. The display itself is like a television – it needs a continuous signal. The Graphics Adaptor creates this signal. The program only sends instructions to the adaptor when it needs to make changes to the display.

Modern graphics adaptors can be very powerful. This lets the program create complex images by sending relatively simple and quick instructions to the adaptor. This is a big advantage for game programs but even the simplest graphics adaptor is sufficient for web browsing, word processing and other office-type programs.

2.12 The USB thumbdrive and printer

You'll want to connect a printer to your computer so that you can print out your documents. You may also have a USB thumbdrive / Data Stick available so that you can save copies of your documents and move them to a different computer. Even the smallest and cheapest thumbdrive sold now will be adequate for this.

We can now return to the question at the start of this chapter: what does all the gobbledegook about that computer mean:

- An Intel Dual Core 3.3GHz processor. This is the CPU micro-chip. It runs at 3.3 Gigahertz (3,300,000,000 steps per second) and has two CPUs internally so it can do two operations simultaneously.

- 4GB of RAM. 4 Gigabytes of RAM can store 4,294,967,296 bytes, equivalent to nearly 7000 miles of paper tape. It can hold many programs and other data at the same time. They won't need to be copied to and from the hard disk as often which speeds things up.

- A 500GB hard drive. The hard disk could theoretically hold 500,000,000,000 bytes, equivalent to nearly 800,000 miles of paper tape

- An Intel HD2000 Graphics adapter – you might want something better if you plan to play computer action games.

- Windows 7 – Microsoft's current version. You'll be installing Ubuntu but can keep Windows too.

This would be a good computer for demanding tasks such as video editing. If all you want to do is word processing, spreadsheets, e-mail and web-browsing, any modern computer will be more than adequate and you could save some money.

> *In the early days of personal computers, Bill Gates remarked that 640 KB of RAM was all that anyone would ever need. A modern **PC (Personal Computer)** has thousands of times more RAM but still manages to fill it up.*

3 Installing Ubuntu.

You might have a computer with Ubuntu already installed but it's unlikely. Most computers have Microsoft Windows installed.

*We'll use Windows to download and install Ubuntu. We'll use the **WUBI** (Windows UBuntu Installer) version because:*

- *It's easy to install it on a Windows computer.*

- *After it's installed, you can choose to use it or Windows whenever you start the computer.*

- *If you decide Ubuntu isn't for you, it's easy to remove it.*

3.1 Clicking and dragging with the mouse or touchpad

When you move the mouse or drag your finger over the touchpad, you'll see a **cursor** move on the screen. This is the **mouse cursor** – it may be an arrow, a hand or I-shaped and may change as it moves about. When we talk of **clicking** somewhere or on something, this means moving the cursor to that place on the screen, then pressing the left hand button on the mouse briefly.

Instead of using the left mouse button, you can click with the right hand one. This is **right-clicking** and usually has a different effect from normal clicking.

Clicking the left mouse button twice in quick succession is called **double-clicking**. If you click too slowly, the computer sees your clicks as two normal ones – double clicking has a different effect from this. Sometimes, you need to click three or four times in quick succession: **triple-clicking** or **quadruple-clicking**.

If you keep the left hand button held down and move the cursor, this is called **dragging**. It can be used to move various things around on the screen. They end up in the position that they are when you release the button.

It's possible to change settings on the computer so that the mouse buttons are switched. This may suit left-handed people better. With that setting, clicking and dragging uses the right button and right-clicking uses the left button.

3.2 Starting the Windows 7 Web Browser

The procedure if you have Vista will be only slightly different. If you have Windows XP, follow Section 3.3.

Turn the computer on. Click on 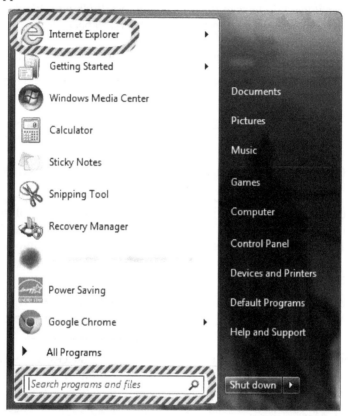 at the bottom left of the screen. A box appears.

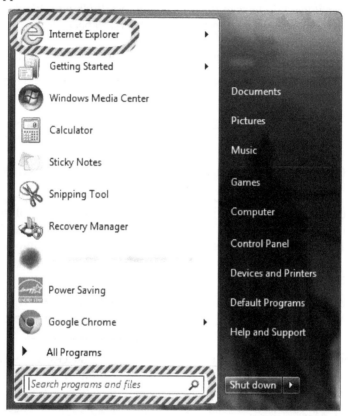

You'll usually see your choice of Windows web browser program as circled at the top. If this is Microsoft Internet Explorer as shown here, you can just click on it.

Instead, it might be an alternative browser such as Firefox or Chrome. These do the same job but some things won't match in the steps that follow.

If you want Internet Explorer, click in the Search programs and files box (also circled) and start typing Internet Explorer. As you type, the list of programs above the box changes. Once you see Internet Explorer in the list, click on it.

A window appears on the screen.

In this case, you're seeing the Google search page. Your web browser might start up with a different or blank page. Don't worry.

Near the top left of the Internet Explorer window is a box where you can type the address of a web page. It's circled in the picture above.

Click in the box. All the text in it changes colour – it's highlighted. If this doesn't work, try double or triple-clicking. Type *www.ubuntu.com*. This automatically replaces the highlighted text. Press RETURN (the large key at the right side of the keyboard with a left-facing arrow – it may also say ENTER). The Ubuntu home page loads into Internet Explorer.

3.3 Starting the Windows XP Web Browser

If you're using Vista or Windows 7, you've already loaded the Ubuntu home page. Skip this section.

Click on **start** at the bottom left of the screen. A box appears.

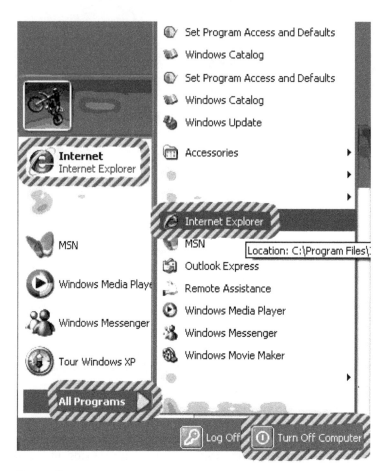

You'll usually see your choice of Windows web browser program as circled at the middle left. If this is Microsoft Internet Explorer as shown here, you can just click on it.

Instead, it might be an alternative browser such as Firefox or Chrome. These do the same job but some things won't match in the steps that follow.

If you want Internet Explorer, move the mouse pointer over All Programs (circled at bottom left). A list of programs appears as shown here. Click on Internet Explorer in the list (circled at middle right).

A window appears on the screen.

In this case you're seeing the Google search page. Your web browser might start up with a different or blank page. Don't worry.

Near the top left of the Internet Explorer window is a box where you can type the address of a web page. It's circled in the picture above.

Click in the box. All the text in it changes colour – it's highlighted. If this doesn't work, try double or triple-clicking. Type *www.ubuntu.com*. This automatically replaces the highlighted text. Press RETURN (the large key at the right side of the keyboard with a left-facing arrow – it may also say ENTER). The Ubuntu home page loads into Internet Explorer.

3.4 Downloading and installing Ubuntu

Look for Get Ubuntu now on the Ubuntu home page. Move the mouse cursor over it and click. A different web page appears.

If you don't see Get Ubuntu now *, it might be lower down on the page. Click ⌄ or ▾ (circled above) repeatedly until you see it.*

The Ubuntu home page may have changed by the time you do this. You might need to guess a bit...

Look for *Check out the Windows Installer*. Click on it. Another web page appears.

Look for **Start download** and click on it.

If nothing seems to happen, look for a message like this just above the web page:

To help protect your security, Internet Explorer blocked this site from downloading files to your computer. Click here for options...

If you see this, click on it and click *Download File...* in the box that appears.

You may see another box asking *Do you want to run or save this file?*. Click [Run]. The file containing the first part of the installer program **downloads** from the Ubuntu website and is saved on the hard disk of your computer.

> *In Chapter 6, you'll see that a file is just a series of bytes of data.*

You may see yet another box asking *Do you want to run this software?*. Click [Run] or [Yes].

> *Internet Explorer asks all these questions about whether to download and run the program because it's trying to protect you from unwittingly downloading malware (Section 2.6) from a dubious website. The questions may vary a bit depending on your version of Windows and how it's configured.*

> *The Ubuntu site isn't dubious and you can safely download and run the installer. Of course you must be cautious when you're viewing other web sites.*

The installer program starts running and a window appears:

*This is the XP version. The Vista and Windows 7 versions are
slightly different but not enough to be a problem.*

The top box on the left side shows the disk drive that the installer is
planning to use and the free space on it (10 GB in the picture above).
The *Installation size:* box just below shows the amount of this space
that the installer is planning to use for Ubuntu. You can change this by
clicking ⌄ to its right, then clicking on a different amount in the list
that appears.

*You want to have enough disk space to add programs and save
documents in Ubuntu but you should leave some free space for
Windows too. Depending whether you expect to mostly use
Ubuntu or Windows, you may want to increase Installation size:
(giving more space to Ubuntu) or decrease it (keeping more
space for Windows).*

The top box on the right hand side sets the language that will be used
for menus, help screens, etc. in Ubuntu. If it's wrong, click ⌄ to its
right and click on the correct language in the list that appears. If you
can't see it, use the up and down arrow keys to move through the list.

*This book shows the names of keys on the keyboard in capitals.
BACKSPACE is usually a large key above RETURN with a left-*

pointing arrow. The wide SPACEBAR is below the letter keys. ALT is to its left. TAB is near the top left: it may be marked with arrows pointing to left and right. ESC (Escape) should be at the top left. DELETE (or DEL) should be somewhere near the right hand side of the keyboard. There may be CTRL (Control) and SHIFT keys on both sides of the SPACEBAR: you can use the one on either side, whichever is more convenient. The SHIFT keys may only be marked with upward pointing arrows.

*There are also four keys close together near the right-hand side of the keyboard that are marked with arrows pointing up, down, left and right. These are the **arrow keys**.*

The *Username:* box underneath should already be filled in with your Windows user name (blurred out above). If you want to use a different name in Ubuntu, click after the name, press BACKSPACE several times to get rid of it, then type the name you want to use.

Choose a log-in password and make a note of it. Type the password into the topmost box under *Password:* then type it again into the lower box. Click [Install].

Ubuntu normally requires you to use a password to log in. It's possible to change things later on so you can log in without one but the password is also used to protect confidential information such as the passphrases for wireless networks.

For security, the password you type in isn't shown. If you make a typing mistake, the two boxes won't match and you'll see an error message when you click [Install]. Use BACKSPACE repeatedly to clear the password in both boxes, retype it and click [Install] again.

You might again be asked whether to download or run programs. Answer as before. You see:

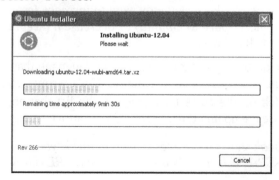

Ubuntu is downloaded and installed, complete with LibreOffice. This takes at least a few minutes, perhaps longer. You can go away and do something else until you see this:

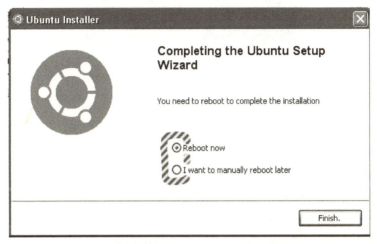

Note the two small circles that are circled. You want the top one alongside *Reboot now* to be filled in. If it isn't filled as shown here, click on it. Click [Finish.].

> *The two circles are known as **Radio buttons**. Some dialogues have more than two of them in a group. Like the station buttons on a car radio and unlike tickboxes (Section 5.5), only one can be selected at a time – the previous choice is automatically cleared.*

The computer shuts down, then restarts. You see something like this:

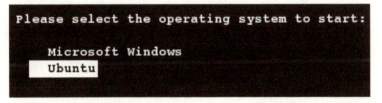

Press the up or down arrow key as needed so that Ubuntu is highlighted as shown, then press RETURN.

> *Ubuntu may restart immediately and you might not see this screen until the next time you start the computer.*

Ubuntu starts. After a longer than normal delay while it sets itself up for the first time, you see something like this:

Type the password that you chose earlier and press RETURN. After a few seconds, you see the Ubuntu desktop as shown at the start of Chapter 4 and you can begin working with it.

WUBI may not work correctly with some computers for various reasons. If you find yourself stuck here, perhaps you can find someone who can help you install Ubuntu as described in Section 3.7.

What you learned:

- *What downloading is.*
- *Where various keys are on the keyboard.*
- *What radio buttons are.*

3.5 Starting Ubuntu or Windows

In future, when you start your computer, you'll see the *Please select the operating system to start:* message shown above. Either Windows or Ubuntu is highlighted and starts automatically after a while. It'll start immediately if you press RETURN.

Instead, you can use the up or down arrow key to highlight the other choice and and press RETURN to start it.

When you choose to start Ubuntu, you may see a further screen where you can select the version you want to run. This tends to appear once Ubuntu has been updated (Section 12.8). The newest version is already highlighted and starts automatically after a few seconds. You can start it immediately by pressing RETURN.

- If you start Windows, it behaves just as it did before you installed Ubuntu. It will have less free disk space though because WUBI is using some of it.

- If you start Ubuntu, you'll see the same screen as above where you need to enter your password. Do this and press RETURN.

3.6 Ubuntu versions

A new version of Ubuntu is released each April and October. A version is given a number consisting of the year, a dot and the month (04 for April or 10 for October). Each version also has a name consisting of the name of an animal and an adjective starting with the same letter as the animal's name. The letters are in alphabetic order.

*For example, the version just released at the time of writing (April 2012) is **12.04 Precise Pangolin**. The previous version, released in October 2011, was 11.10 Oneiric Ocelot.*

There are at least a few minor changes in each new version, including changes to LibreOffice. This book uses Ubuntu 12.04 with LibreOffice 3.5 and you may find some differences if you've installed another version. I hope these don't cause you too much trouble.

3.7 Other ways to install Ubuntu

You can install Ubuntu in a separate disk partition from a magazine cover DVD or by downloading the installer from www.ubuntu.com and burning a DVD. If your computer doesn't have a DVD drive, you can copy the installer to a thumbdrive.

Ubuntu runs more reliably and slightly faster when it's installed on a separate disk partition. You'll still be able to use Windows.

There are instructions for all these steps on the Ubuntu website. You can find instructions elsewhere for moving your existing WUBI installation to a separate partition. However, it's all tricky and a bit dangerous – there's lots of jargon involved and it's too easy to destroy the Windows installation on your computer.

Once you've worked your way through this book, particularly Chapters 4, 6 and 12, you'll be in a much better position to consider doing one of these things.

4 Basics of Ubuntu

This chapter covers basics such as how to start and close programs, manage their windows and switch between them.

You may need to start Ubuntu as described in Section 3.5. After a short delay, you see something like this:

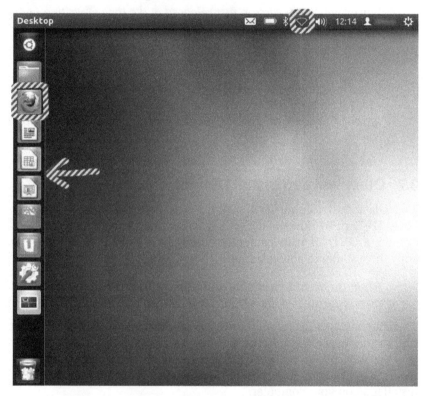

*This is a **screenshot**. It's been changed to add candy stripe markings around important things and to blur out irrelevant ones. Section 10.2 shows how you can add screenshots to your documents.*

*Most computers have a **network** connection allowing them to communicate over the internet, e.g. so you can browse web pages. They can also communicate with other computers and printers connected to the same LAN (Local Area Network).*

If you have a wireless network (WiFi) adapter (e.g. if you're using a laptop or netbook), you'll see *(circled) near the top right. Click on it. A list of nearby wireless networks appears. Click on the name (SSID) of the one you want to use. If it's encrypted, you'll be asked for the passphrase. The person who set up the network knows this. Type it in and press RETURN.*

The network connection is made and *changes to* . *You're now able to use the web browser, e-mail, etc.*

The number of bright arcs over the dot in *shows the signal strength: it decreases as you move away from the network access point or router.*

Ubuntu remembers network names and passphrases. Next time you start it, it'll look for a name that it knows and connect automatically. You'll only see *again if you're out of range of any network that Ubuntu recognises. You can click* *and connect to a new network: previous networks that you've used are still remembered.*

If your network connection uses a cable, you'll see *instead of* *or* *and the connection should work right away.*

Most of the screen is occupied by the **desktop**. At the left hand side is the **Launcher** (arrowed). It contains **icons** for programs that you're likely to use and for programs that are currently running on the computer.

If you leave the computer unused for some time, the screen may go completely dark. This is a power saving and security feature. Press any key on the keyboard to bring the computer back to life – you may be asked for your password again.

What you learned:

- **What the Launcher and desktop are.**
- **What an icon is.**
- *What a network is.*
- *How to connect to a wireless network.*
- *That connection to a wired network happens automatically.*
- *What to do if the screen goes dark.*

4.1 Starting the Web Browser

Although this book doesn't cover using the web in depth, it's something you're likely to want to do. This section gets you started with Firefox but, more importantly, it shows you how to start a program and some of the things to look for in its window.

Click on the ![icon] icon (circled) on the Launcher. The computer copies the **Firefox** web browser program from the hard disk into its RAM and starts running it. A **window** appears on the screen.

At the top of the window is the **titlebar** showing the name of the program (*Mozilla Firefox*) and the document or web site that is open. At the left hand end of the titlebar are three on-screen **buttons** (circled). Clicking ⊗ would close (end) the program – don't click it now.

Google (www.google.com) is the best known and most popular ***search engine***. *Ubuntu and Firefox have a deal with Google where their search box appears as shown here when you start Firefox.*

Your web browser might start up with a different or blank page. Don't worry.

It may be that, on your computer, the web page looks a bit different and occupies most of the screen with the title appearing at the very top left of the screen. Move the mouse cursor over the title. The three buttons appear. Click on ⊜.

Near the top left of the Firefox window is a box where you can type the address of a web page. It's circled in the picture above and is showing *about:startpage*.

Double-click in the box. All the text in it changes colour – it's high-lighted. Type *www.bing.com*. This automatically replaces the highlighted text. Press RETURN (the large key at the right side of the keyboard with a left-facing arrow – it may also say ENTER). The Bing search page loads into Firefox.

> *Bing is Microsoft's equivalent to Google (even though you're using Ubuntu, you can use any search engine you want). Both Google and Bing search pages feature a box where you can type a question or just some words, then press RETURN. A list of web pages found on the Internet is shown and you can click on the underlined **link** for any of them to view it. In general, these pages aren't controlled by either Google or Bing: there's no guarantee of their quality, truthfulness or freedom from malware.*

> *When you click on a link on any web page, the address in the circled box changes to that of the new page. If you already know the address of a web page, you can just type it directly into the box and press RETURN.*

> *You can return to pages you were viewing previously by clicking* ⇐ *(circled). Further details of using the web are outside the scope of this book.*

What you learned:

- **How to start the Firefox web browser.**
- **What a window is.**
- **Where the window titlebar is and what it shows.**
- **How to go to a web site by typing in its address.**
- *How to quickly return to a web page you viewed previously.*
- *How to use a search engine such as Google or Bing.*

4.2 Managing program windows

Click on ⊖ (one of the three circled buttons). The Firefox window disappears. There's a small arrow to the left of 🦊 in the Launcher. Firefox is still running but has been **minimised**. Thanks to a technique called **multitasking**, other programs can run at the same time – you could start another one (e.g. LibreOffice Writer) now.

Click 🦊 on the Launcher. The Firefox window reappears.

> *Each program that's running appears on the Launcher and you can switch to it by clicking on its icon. If you click on the icon of a program that isn't minimised but is partly or completely hidden by another window, its window is brought to the front. If you can't see the window for your program, try clicking its icon on the Launcher again.*

Place the cursor at the bottom right corner of the Firefox window. It should change to an arrow pointing into a corner. Hold down the left mouse/trackpad button then, keeping it held down, drag the corner so that the window becomes smaller or larger. This is **resizing**: the window stays at the new size when you release the button.

You can place the cursor over any corner or side of the window and drag that corner or side to change the size and shape of the window. Make sure for now that it isn't filling the whole screen.

Now place the cursor over the titlebar at the top of the window away from the three buttons. Hold down the left mouse button and move the cursor. The window is dragged. Release the button: the window stays at its new position.

> *By adjusting the size and position of their windows, you can see and use more than one program at the same time.*
>
> *Sometimes, a window moves upwards until you can't see its titlebar or the three buttons any more. Place the mouse cursor over the part of the window that you can see, hold down the ALT key, then drag downwards to move the window until its titlebar is visible again.*
>
> *If you click 🗖 on the Launcher, the screen shrinks to ¼ size and you see three more blank ¼ size screens. These are different **workspaces**. You can organise your running programs by*

dragging some onto different workspaces, then switch between them by clicking ▣ *and double-clicking on the one you want.*

You may not find that workspaces are particularly useful but sometimes a program unexpectedly moves itself to a different one (a bug). If a program's window fails to appear when you click its icon on the Launcher, click ▣ *to see if that's what's happened.*

The web page may not all fit in the window. If so, scroll bars appear at the right hand and bottom of the window. These are marked with arrows in the previous picture. If the window on your computer doesn't have these scroll bars, make it smaller until they appear.

The scroll bar at the right side lets you move the web page up and down in the window by clicking on the arrows at each end, by dragging the large button between them up and down or by clicking on the area below (or above) the large button. Experiment with it.

The scroll bar at the bottom works the same way. It lets you move the web page from side to side in the window.

Click ▣ (another of the three circled buttons). The window fills the screen with its title on the bar at the top and the three buttons disappear. The window is **maximised**. You'll usually want the window for your word processor or spreadsheet to be like this so you can see as much as possible of your document unless you're working with another program or document at the same time.

Move the cursor over the bar at the very top of the screen. The three buttons appear there. Click ▣. The window is no longer maximised – you can resize and move it again.

> *Other programs including the LibreOffice ones have windows that work the same way as the Firefox one. They also have the titlebar, the three buttons and they may have scrollbars.*

Click on ⓧ. If you started any other programs, close them the same way. The programs stop running and the RAM they were using is freed.

What you learned:

- **How to minimise a window.**
- **How to resize and move windows.**
- **What scrollbars do and how to use them.**
- **How to maximise and restore a window.**

- **How to run more than one program at a time and use the Launcher to switch between them.**

- **How to close (stop) a program.**

4.3 Turning the computer off

When you've finished using the computer you should turn it off correctly so that all documents, settings, etc. are saved.

Click ⚙ at the top right of the screen. A list appears.

- You can click *Shut Down...* in the list to shut the computer down completely. A box appears. Click `Shut Down`. Next time you start the computer, you'll have to wait while it goes through the boot-up process. Then you'll have to reopen any documents you were working on.

- You can click *Suspend* in the list to shut down the CPU and most other parts of the computer, keeping programs and open documents in the RAM. When you start the computer again, it's ready to use in a few seconds but, until then, it continues drawing a small amount of power (e.g. from its battery if it's a laptop) to keep the RAM working. If power is lost or the battery runs down, you could lose recent changes to the documents. It's wise to save them before suspending the computer.

- You can click *Hibernate* in the list to **hibernate** the computer. This is like *Suspend* but *Hibernate* saves data in the RAM to a special part of the hard disk so the computer can fully power down. It's slower to start up again than with *Suspend* but still much quicker than if you turned the computer off completely and had to restart it and reopen your documents.

  Suspend and Hibernate may not appear in the list or may not work properly on some computers. They are more likely to work if Ubuntu is moved to a separate disk partition (Section 3.7).

  When a computer comes with Windows already installed, the manufacturer sets it up to match that type of computer. Ubuntu has to cope with many different computers without tweaking. It doesn't always get things completely right.

What you learned:

- **How to turn off the computer correctly and why you should always do this.**

- *How to suspend or hibernate the computer and what these do.*

- *Why Ubuntu can't always set itself up exactly right for your computer.*

5 Basics of word processing

This chapter shows how to type text into a new document, make changes to it, do some basic formatting, save the document on the hard disk and print it. You'll also learn some important concepts, terms and techniques.

Although you'll be using LibreOffice Writer, most of the steps covered in this chapter are similar for other word processor programs. This includes older versions of Microsoft Word. Word 2010 replaces the drop-down menus with the "ribbon" interface. It has the same functions in a different format.

The document made in this chapter will be used again in Chapter 11.

5.1 Starting LibreOffice Writer

Click 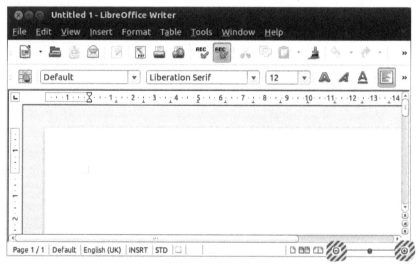 on the Launcher. The LibreOffice Writer program is copied from the hard disk into RAM. There may be a few seconds delay before it starts running and a window appears on the screen.

There's all or part of a white page on a grey background in the Writer window below the ruler. The page may be too large or too small to see comfortably. If so, click repeatedly on one of the circled **zoom** buttons to make it bigger or smaller. ⊕ makes it bigger, ⊖ makes it smaller.

You can also drag the slider between the two buttons. Zooming doesn't change the size of the page itself, only how big it looks on the screen.

You might need to use the scrollbars to see the correct part of the page.

What you learned:

- **How to start Writer.**
- **How to change the size of the page on the screen by zooming.**

5.2 Typing, copying and pasting text

Click anywhere on the blank page. There should be a flashing vertical line near the top left. This is the **text cursor** which shows where anything you type will go.

Type *The quick brown fox jumps over the lazy dog.* (with the final period/full stop). We'll be referring to a sequence of letters like this as **text**.

The sentence, including the period at its end, is stored as a series of bytes in your computer's RAM. If you pulled out the computer's power plug now (don't try it), it would be lost.

Press SPACEBAR once, then move the mouse cursor to the right of the sentence you just typed, hold down the left mouse button and drag the cursor leftwards to the beginning of the sentence.

The sentence, including the space at the end, is highlighted: its background colour is different from the rest of the page. The **highlighting** shows that it's **selected**.

Click on *Edit* (circled), then on *Copy* in the **drop-down menu** that appears.

If you don't see *Edit,* move the mouse cursor over the document title at the very top of the screen. The menu names appear in place of the title.

> *With Ubuntu Unity, menu names such as Edit should be on the bar at the very top of the screen and (like the three buttons) should only appear when you move the mouse cursor over it. At the time of writing, this isn't working correctly with LibreOffice and its menu names appear separately as shown here.*

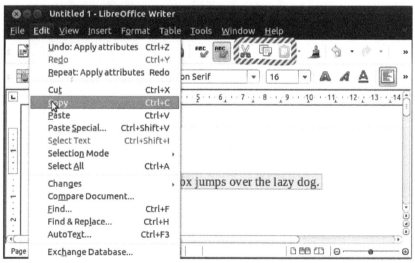

The highlighted text is copied to the **clipboard**.

> *Imagine making a copy of a paper tape containing the highlighted words.*

Notice *Ctrl+C* next to the word *Copy*. This is a **keyboard shortcut**. Pressing these keys together does the same as going to the drop-down Edit menu and clicking on *Copy*. *Ctrl+V* is shown next to the word *Paste* just below.

You can use that keyboard shortcut now to save time. Hold down the CTRL key and press V five times.

> *The first time you press CTRL+V, it removes the highlighted text, puts a copy of the text on the clipboard in its place and places the text cursor at the end of it. In this case, the text was replaced with a copy of itself but the highlighting was removed. You could do the same thing by moving the mouse cursor to the end of the highlighted text and clicking.*

> *The next four times you press CTRL+V, another copy is inserted at the cursor position.*

> *Underneath the list of drop-down menus (e.g. Edit) is a **toolbar** containing icons. Three of these are circled above.*

> *Instead of using the Edit menu or the keyboard shortcuts, you can click on ▤ to copy highlighted text to the clipboard and click on ▣ to paste the text.*

> *There are often several ways to do something. It's easy to find something in a drop-down menu but quicker to click on a toolbar icon such as ▤ and even quicker to use a keyboard shortcut if you remember what it is.*

Release the CTRL key and press RETURN twice. The text cursor moves down. Type *What do these dogs like?*.

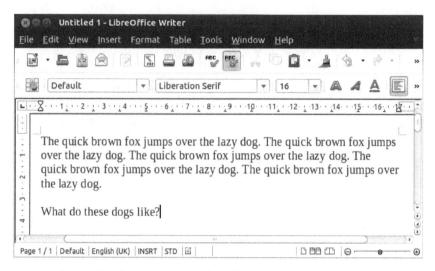

Why is this document such drivel? It's so you don't have to spend much time typing it in and you won't be distracted thinking about what it says and how you could improve it.

What you learned:

- **How to start typing a document.**
- **How to select (highlight) text by dragging with the mouse.**
- **How to use a drop-down menu.**
- **How to copy selected text to the clipboard.**
- **What keyboard shortcuts are.**
- **What *Press CTRL+V* means.**
- **How to paste text from the clipboard.**
- *What a toolbar is.*
- *That any existing highlighted text is replaced with pasted text.*
- *That there are often several ways to do something.*

5.3 Drop-down menus

You saw how, when you click on *Edit*, a drop-down menu appears and you can choose a particular editing operation such as *Copy*. In future, we'll just say something like *Click Edit > Copy*. This means to look for *Edit* in the menus, click on it, then click on *Copy* in the drop down menu that appears.

Sometimes additional submenus appear when you move the mouse cursor over an item in a drop down menu. For example, if you see *Click Insert > Fields > Time*, this means to click on the *Insert* menu, move the mouse cursor over *Fields*, then click on *Time* in the submenu that appears. You can try this, then press BACKSPACE to remove the field.

5.4 Making changes

You saw that the flashing text cursor (a vertical line) appears at the position where anything you type will go.

You can place it by moving the mouse cursor to the position you want and clicking. Try this to place the flashing cursor after the word *jumps* in the first sentence.

You can also use the four arrow keys (Section 3.4) to move the flashing text cursor. Press the one pointing to the right several times to move the cursor past the word *over*.

Press DELETE three times. Each time you press the key, Writer removes one letter from your document and moves all the ones after it back one place. You could imagine snipping a row of holes out of a paper tape and gluing it back together but the computer does this so quickly it seems instantaneous.

You should have got rid of the word *the* but you might have got rid of a space and the *t* and *h* instead so that you see the word *overe*. It depends whether you started with the cursor before or after the space. If the *e* is still there, press DELETE again to get rid of it, then press SPACEBAR to restore the space that you accidentally deleted.

Type *some*. Writer inserts the word *some* into the document at the position of the cursor.

> *You can add text to your document any time you want to. Just put the text cursor where you want it to go and start typing.*
>
> *Somewhere near the right side of the keyboard is a key labelled INSERT. Pressing this switches between **Insert** and **Overwrite** mode. In overwrite mode, anything you type replaces the next letter rather than inserting what you type before it. If you find this is happening, look for INSERT. Maybe you accidentally pressed it. Just press it again.*

You changed a word in the first sentence but it's still wrong. Press BACKSPACE four times. Just like DELETE, it deletes a letter each time you press it but it's the letter before the text cursor instead of the one after it.

Type *a*. Now the sentence is what you want: *The quick brown fox jumps over a lazy dog.*

What you learned:

- **How to reposition the text (flashing) cursor with the mouse.**
- **How to move the text cursor using the arrow keys.**
- **The computer inserts and deletes letters at the position of the text cursor.**
- **BACKSPACE deletes the letter before the text cursor.**
- **DELETE deletes the letter after the text cursor.**
- *You can accidentally switch to overwrite mode. Pressing INSERT fixes this.*

5.5 Finding and replacing

You changed the first sentence to read *a lazy dog*. You could change the next four sentences the same way but computers are supposed to make things easier.

Move the mouse cursor (not the flashing text cursor) over the offending *the* in the second sentence and double-click. The word becomes high-lighted (its background colour changes). Double-clicking automatically selects a whole word.

Click *Edit > Find & Replace....* A dialogue box appears (as shown later on).

> *Remember, this means to click to open the Edit drop-down menu, then click on Find & Replace.*

> *A **dialogue box** is a small to medium sized window that opens when you're doing certain things. It shows information and may allow you to make various choices before clicking on a button to continue what you're doing.*

In *Search for* in the dialogue box, the word *the* is highlighted – that's the text that it's ready to look for. If you wanted, you could type something different or edit the text.

Click on the tickbox next to *Match case* so that a tick appears as shown below, then click in the *Replace with* box and type *a*.

*A dialogue box can have multiple **tickboxes** enabling various options. You can tick any combination of these depending on what you want to happen. This is different from Radio buttons (Section 3.4). Clicking again in a box that's ticked clears it.*

Writer is now ready to search through our document, replacing *the* with *a* when it finds it. Because you ticked *Match case,* it won't change *The* at the start of each sentence. Put the mouse cursor over the *Find & Replace* dialogue box's titlebar and drag the box so that you can see the text in the document.

Click ⎣ Replace ⎦. This changes the highlighted *the* to *a* and highlights the next *the.*

Click ⎣ Replace ⎦ again. This changes it to *a* and highlights the next *the.* Suppose you don't want to change that one. Click ⎣ Find ⎦. LibreOffice leaves it unchanged and highlights the one after.

You can, of course, use Find & Replace without putting anything in the Replace with box if you just want to find a particular word or name in your document.

Let's be brave and click ⎣ Replace All ⎦. That changes any remaining words *the* to *a.*

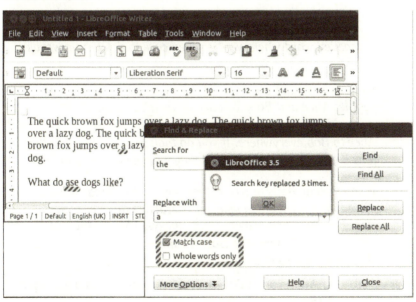

Uh-oh. Writer changed *the* in places you wanted to leave unchanged and it also changed *the* in the word *these* so it now reads *ase.* You could have avoided the last unwanted change by also ticking *Whole words only* or by adding a space at the end of *the* but it's too late now.

Click on [OK], then on [Close] to close the *Find & Replace* box.

Click *Edit > Undo*. If you prefer, just press the shortcut key which is CTRL+Z.

Writer remembers each change that you make to your document. **Undo** undoes them one by one. You've undone the changes you made when you clicked [Replace All]. Don't bother trying to redo them.

> *There's a limit to how many changes you can undo but it's generous. If you accidentally undo more changes than you intended, you can **redo** them by clicking Edit > Redo. Unfortunately you can only redo changes in the same order you made them originally: there isn't a way to skip some of them.*
>
> [Replace All] *is always a dangerous button to click. If you haven't carefully thought out all the possible places that something might match the Search for text, unexpected things can get changed too. In a long document, you might not spot this until it was too late to undo the changes. All the same,* [Replace All] *saves time if you need to make a lot of changes in the document and the Search for text is unusual (e.g. a misspelled word where you've taken care to tick Whole words only).*
>
> *Suppose you have a document describing the duties of two people: Alice and Bob. You decide their roles should be swapped. You can't just start by using* [Replace All] *to change Alice to Bob everywhere. If you do that, Bob will have all the jobs and* [Replace All] *could only give them all to Alice.*
>
> *What you can do is to use* [Replace All] *to change the word Alice to a nonsense sequence of characters that never occur elsewhere in your document, e.g. abcxyz. You can then use* [Replace All] *to change Bob to Alice and finally use it again to change abcxyz to Bob.*

Press CTRL+A. All the text in the document is selected and highlighted. Press SPACEBAR.

Oops. What happened?

The text you just selected (the whole document in this case) was replaced with a single space. Don't panic. *Edit > Undo* or CTRL+Z undoes that mistake too.

What you learned:

- **How to quickly select (highlight) a word.**
- **How to move a dialogue box by dragging.**
- **What tickboxes are and how you can tick and clear them.**
- **That Writer can search for a particular sequence of letters, e.g. a word, part of a word or a phrase (several words with spaces in between).**
- **That Writer can quickly and easily replace that sequence with something different.**
- **That Writer can do this everywhere in your document in an instant.**
- **That the computer does exactly what you tell it to do, even if that isn't what you wanted.**
- **You can undo recent changes to your document if something goes wrong.**
- **This includes the heart-stopping case where your document disappears completely because you accidentally replaced it all with a single space.**
- *What a dialogue box is.*
- *You can redo changes if you accidentally undo too many of them.*
- *How to use* Replace All *to swap two words such as names.*

5.6 Selecting

You've seen a number of ways to select words in a document. Selecting is something you'll do often and it's useful to know how to do it quickly and easily.

- You can select text in a document by placing the mouse cursor at one end of it, then holding down the left mouse button and dragging to the other end of the selection.
- You can select everything in a document with *Edit > Select All* or by pressing CTRL+A.

- In Writer, double-clicking selects a word, triple-clicking selects a whole sentence and quadruple-clicking selects a whole paragraph. Other programs may be slightly different but you can always try different clicks and see what happens.

After you've selected something, you can **extend** the selection by holding down SHIFT and clicking where you want the selection to start or end. For example, suppose you want to select several pages of a document. You can't see them all on the screen at the same time and selecting by dragging with the mouse is tricky. Instead, select the first word you want on the first page, then use the scroll bar to go to and see the last word you want in the selection. While holding down SHIFT, click just after it.

There are many things you can do with a selection. You can delete it using either the DELETE or BACKSPACE key. You can replace it with whatever is on the clipboard using *Edit > Paste* or CTRL+V. You can also replace selected text by typing something new.

You can put a selection on the clipboard with *Edit > Cut* (CTRL+X) or *Edit > Copy* (CTRL+C). **Cut** moves the selection to the clipboard. **Copy** leaves the selection in place and puts a new copy on the clipboard.

You can also click ✂ on the toolbar to cut the selection.

What you learned:

- **Things can be selected by dragging over them or, in many cases, clicking on them.**
- **You can extend a selection by holding down SHIFT and clicking.**
- **You can select everything in the document using *Edit > Select All* or CTRL+A.**
- **You can delete a selection with DELETE or BACKSPACE.**
- **The difference between cutting and copying something to the clipboard.**

There are many more things you can do with selections that you'll be seeing later on.

5.7 Paragraphs, margins, indents and tabs

Before you typed the last line of our document, you pressed the

RETURN key twice. Pressing RETURN tells Writer to start a new paragraph. Pressing it twice made Writer put a paragraph consisting of a completely blank line between our two paragraphs. This makes it easy to see where the second paragraph starts.

Section 7.4 shows another way to add space between paragraphs.

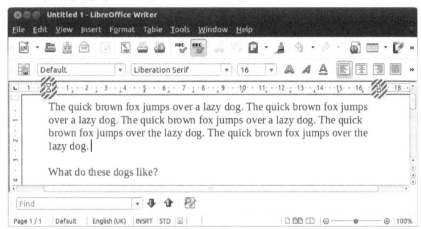

At each end of the **ruler** above the document, there are small sliders circled above. Place the text cursor anywhere in the first paragraph, then try dragging the sliders along the ruler.

If you don't see the ruler, click the View menu and click on Ruler so that a tick mark appears to its left.

The slider at the right hand end sets the right margin. As it's dragged to the left, lines of text in the first paragraph get shorter.

The top slider at the left sets the starting position for the first line in the paragraph. Dragging the bottom slider at the left sets the starting position for the remaining lines in the paragraph.

There's also a ruler at the left hand side. Numbers on the rulers show distances on the printed page (they may be different on the screen). Screenshots in this book have the rulers set to show distances in centimetres. If you right-click anywhere on a ruler, you can choose the units from a list that appears. E.g. you can make the rulers show distances in inches.

If you drag the bottom left slider away from the left-hand end of the ruler, you can position the top left slider to its left. This **outdents** the first line of the paragraph – something you might occasionally want to do.

The sliders are only affecting the first paragraph because that's where you put the text cursor. If you had selected all or part of a number of paragraphs (or all of them with CTRL+A), the sliders would affect all the selected paragraphs at the same time.

Drag all the sliders back to where they originally were, then drag the top left one to the right to **indent** the paragraph.

Click below the second paragraph. This puts the text cursor just after the question mark. Press TAB and type *Walkies*. Press TAB again and type *Chasing things*. Press RETURN, then TAB, and type *Eating*. Press TAB again and type *Barking*. Press TAB again and type *Sleeping*.

> *Tab is an abbreviation of Tabulator. This is a key on a traditional typewriter that's used when typing a table.*

You can see small ⊥ marks on the ruler. These are default **tab stops**. Each time you pressed TAB, the following word started below the next tab stop.

Drag with the mouse to select part or all of the last two lines. Click on ⊥ above the start of the word *Walkies*. ⊥ changes to ∟ and *Walkies* and *Eating* both start below it. Click on the ruler again a bit to the right of *Walkies*. Another ∟ appears and *Chasing things* and *Barking* both start below it. You've set two tab stops.

> *You can use tabs to arrange text in columns.*

> *There are still default tab stops to the right of the two that you set. Sleeping is lined up with one of them.*

Drag the ∟ marks along the ruler and the text below in both lines moves with them. The lines are separate paragraphs because you pressed RETURN between them but, as when setting indents, tab changes affect all selected paragraphs.

> *To get rid of a tab stop, place the mouse pointer over its ∟ mark, hold down the left mouse button, wait a moment, then drag it down away from the ruler.*

> *When you outdent a paragraph, the bottom left slider also acts as a tab stop. For example, if you're typing a glossary, you can set up outdenting and press TAB after each word that you define. The first word after the TAB lines up with the start of subsequent lines of the definition.*

If you right-click a tab stop on the ruler, you'll see a list of stop types and you can select a different one. With the usual Left stop, the first character following the tab will be aligned with the stop. The other stop types work on all the text you type following the tab up to another tab or the end of the line. A Right stop aligns the end of the text with the stop and a Center stop centres it on the stop. A Decimal stop is similar to a Right stop but, if the text contains a decimal point, it's aligned with the stop. This is used to set up a column of numbers, e.g. prices.

What you learned:

- **Pressing RETURN starts a new paragraph.**
- **How to change the left and right margins.**
- **How to indent or outdent paragraphs.**
- **How to set and adjust tabs to create columns of text.**
- **That, if you don't set tab stops, default tab positions are used.**
- **That margins, indents and outdents and tabs can apply to one, several or all paragraphs in a document.**
- *How to make the rulers appear.*
- *How to change the dimension units on the ruler.*
- *How to remove a tab stop.*
- *An easy way to format a glossary.*
- *The difference between a Left, Right, Center and Decimal tab stop.*

5.8 Word Wrapping and Justification

You'll have noticed, when you adjusted the right margin of the first paragraph of the document, that Writer automatically chose the word beginning each line of the paragraph so that the previous line fitted nicely. This is automatic **word-wrapping**.

The lines in a paragraph are also automatically adjusted when you add or delete text or if you change the text font, which you'll be doing soon.

You can see why you should only press RETURN when you want to start a new paragraph. Not only don't you need to press RETURN at the end of a line within a paragraph, doing it causes problems. Writer treats the next line as a new paragraph and the word-wrapping won't work correctly if you make changes later.

*There are times when you want to start a new line without it starting a new paragraph. Holding down SHIFT and pressing RETURN does this: it's called a **line break**.*

*Holding down CTRL and pressing RETURN starts a new paragraph on a new page. This is known as a **page break**.*

When Writer decides to start a new line in a paragraph, it's unlikely that the previous line will be exactly the right length to extend to the right-hand margin. Usually, it'll be a bit shorter. There are four ways to deal with the leftover space.

The simplest answer is to leave it all at the right hand end of the line. All lines start at the left hand margin but most end a bit before the right-hand one. This is known as **left-justified**: it's what you've used so far.

Things can be reversed so that the leftover space is on the left hand side and all lines end at the right margin. This is **right-justified** text – it isn't used often.

Another option is to split the leftover space equally between the two ends of each line so that the line is **centred** between the margins.

The last option is to add the leftover space equally between words on the line and sometimes also between letters in each word. This allows each line to start at the left margin and end exactly at the right margin too. It's known as **fully-justified** text. Newspapers, magazines and books often use full justification but it can look too formal in other documents.

You've probably spotted that each of these four paragraphs uses the justification that it describes: left, right, centred and full.

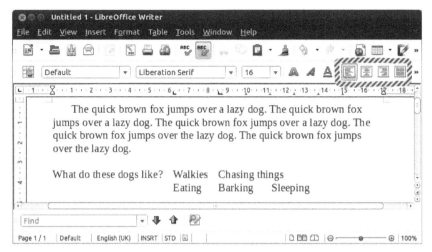

To set the justification for one or more paragraphs, place the cursor there or select the paragraphs, then click one of the four buttons circled in the picture above.

What you learned:

- **How word-wrapping works.**
- **Why you should only press RETURN to start a new paragraph.**
- **What text justification is and how to set it. This includes centring text.**
- *How to start a new line within a paragraph by pressing SHIFT+RETURN.*
- *How to start a new page by pressing CTRL+RETURN.*

5.9 Styles, Typefaces and Fonts

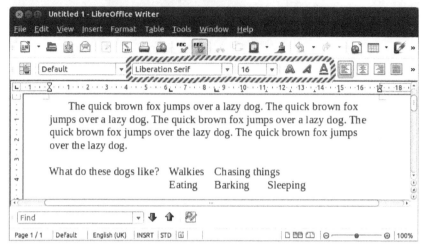

Two drop-down **selector boxes** are circled above along with three **style** buttons to their right.

> *Move the mouse cursor over* ▲ *(one of the style buttons) without clicking it. A small box appears saying Bold (Ctrl+B). Move it over* ▲ *and a box appears saying Italic (Ctrl+I). Move it over* ▲ *and a box appears saying Underline (Ctrl+U). These are **tooltips**: they tell you what the button does and, in this case, they show you the keyboard shortcut you could use instead of clicking on the button.*

> *Many on-screen buttons in various programs have tooltips.*

Drag over the first and second sentences of the first paragraph to select them, then click ▲ or press CTRL+B. The words become darker and more prominent – **the style is now Bold**.

Click the mouse anywhere in the document to unselect the two sentences, then select the first sentence on its own. ▲ is still high-lighted, showing that the words are in bold. Click the button. It's no longer highlighted and the first sentence is back to normal. The second sentence is still in bold.

> *Each time you click one of the three style buttons, the style is either applied to or removed from the selected text.*

Select the third sentence and click ▲ or press CTRL+I. The words are slanting – *the style is Italic*.

Select the fourth sentence and click ▲ or press CTRL+U. <u>The sentence</u>

is underlined.

Select the fifth sentence and click all three buttons in succession. ***The sentence is in bold and italic and it is also underlined***.

> *You can use any combination of the three buttons or any combination of the keyboard shortcuts one after another.*

Drag with the mouse to select the whole of the first paragraph, including the blank line below it. Press CTRL+C to copy it, including the blank line, to the clipboard. Press CTRL+V three times so that there are three copies of the paragraph.

Select the whole of the second copy by dragging with the mouse or by quadruple-clicking in it, then go to the box circled above showing the number *16* (on your screen, it'll probably show 10 or 12). Click ▾ to its right and then on the number *20* in the drop-down list that appears. All the words in the second paragraph get bigger. We changed the paragraph to 20 point.

> *The size of printed characters is traditionally given in **points**, measured from the top of a tall character such as h to the bottom of a descender, e.g. in j. A point is 1/72 of an inch (0.353 mm). 10 point is the smallest size you should normally use – anything smaller could be classed as "fine print" although newspapers often use smaller print and are still quite legible. 12 point is easier to read and you'll want to use larger sizes again for headings, etc.*

> *Writer normally defaults to 10 or 12 point text. Screenshots prepared for this book use 16 point text to make it easier to see.*

Select the third paragraph, then go to the box circled above showing *Liberation Serif*. Click ▾ to its right. A list of **typefaces** installed on your computer appears. There may be too many to show them all. If so, there will be a scrollbar next to the list. Scroll up, find *Liberation Sans* and click on it.

The typeface of the third paragraph changes from Liberation Serif to Liberation Sans.

Liberation Serif is a **serif** typeface – the letters have small lines across their ends.

Liberation Sans is a simpler **sans-serif** typeface.

*Liberation Sans and Liberation Serif are **proportional fonts** –
each letter is just as wide as it needs to be. The widest letter is m,
others such as i are narrower.*

*Another typeface worth mentioning is Courier. This is a mono-
spaced font – all letters are spaced far enough apart for an m to
fit.*

`Courier looks as if it was typed on a typewriter.`

*In traditional printing, a **font** is a box of cast metal letters of a
particular typeface, point size and style (e.g. italic) but people
often say font when they mean typeface. For example, they might
say to use Times New Roman as the font for a document that
contains text of various styles and point sizes.*

*Ubuntu uses its installed fonts to convert the letter codes stored
by programs running on the computer into the shape of the
corresponding letter on the screen or on paper in the printer.
For example, the letter A is stored in memory as a single byte (8
bits) but this code is converted to a pattern of several hundred or
thousand dots to make the shape of an A on the screen or on
paper with a particular typeface, point size and style.*

*Sometimes Ubuntu has different versions of a font installed to
produce the different styles. If not, it modifies the normal style of
the font (e.g. by widening the lines or slanting the characters).*

*You can highlight individual words or even letters within a word
and change their typeface, size and style.*

*As a rule of thumb, you should avoid using more than two or
three different typefaces in the same document. Using too many
looks messy.*

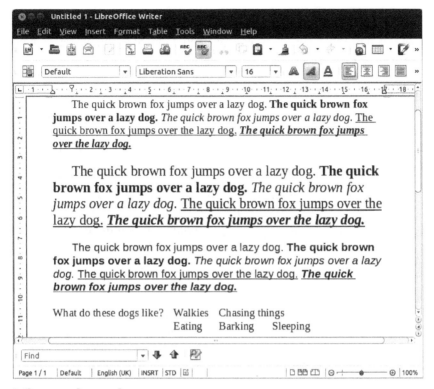

What you learned:

- **What text styles are and how to set and unset them.**
- **That text styles can be used in any combination.**
- **What a typeface is.**
- **How to change the size and typeface of text.**
- **The difference between serif and sans-serif typefaces.**
- *What tooltips are.*
- *The difference between proportional and mono-spaced typefaces.*
- *That text size is measured in points.*
- *What a font is (it can mean two different things) and how the computer uses it.*
- *Not to go overboard with too many different typefaces.*

5.10 Symbols

Ubuntu has fonts such as Dingbats and OpenSymbol which contain symbols like ♥ or ☎ instead of letters. Ordinary fonts such as Liberation Sans include foreign alphabets (e.g. Greek) and some commonly-used symbols such as ©.

To insert a symbol at the text cursor position, click *Insert > Special character....* A dialogue box opens. Choose a font and look for the symbol you want. You may need to try several fonts (e.g. *OpenSymbol*) and scroll down to find it. Click on the symbol, then click OK .

> *Once you have a symbol in your document, you can click just after it and see what font it's from in the typeface selector box. If you need a related symbol it'll probably be available in that font too.*
>
> *You can copy and paste a symbol already in your document anywhere else that you need it.*
>
> *Symbols are stored in memory just like letters: it's the font selection that makes them look different. If you accidentally change the typeface for some of your text to a symbol font such as Dingbats, it'll start showing as meaningless symbols. Don't panic, just change it back.*

What you learned:

- **That Ubuntu has special fonts which contain symbols instead of letters.**
- **That ordinary fonts can include foreign alphabets and some symbols.**
- **How to find and insert the symbols you want into your document.**
- *How to find related symbols that may be available in the same font.*
- *That you can copy and paste symbols.*
- *What happens if you accidentally select a symbol font.*

5.11 Windows fonts

You'll have problems if a document is moved to a different computer that doesn't have a font that you used installed on it. This often happens if you e-mail the document to someone else who uses Windows. Their computer will automatically choose a similar font that it does have installed but the match may not be good. You can avoid this problem by e-mailing the document as a PDF file (Section 7.11).

Section 12.4 shows how to make Windows fonts available in Ubuntu. This lets you use Arial (sans-serif), Times New Roman (serif) and Webdings and Wingdings (symbols) which are usually present on a Windows computer. You can make other Windows fonts available too - some of them are very fancy.

5.12 Non-printing characters

You'll remember that the teleprinter machine in Chapter 2 punched a special pattern of holes in the tape when the spacebar was pressed and that this moved the print position on by one place without printing anything when the words on the tape were printed. Other special patterns would be punched if the TAB or RETURN keys were pressed. Your computer stores these same patterns as special characters (bytes) in its memory when you press those keys.

Two different special characters can be stored when the RETURN key is pressed. Carriage Return (CR) tells a teleprinter to move its printing position to the start of the line and Line Feed (LF) tells it to advance the paper to a new line. Windows stores the CR-LF sequence when RETURN is pressed while Unix-based systems including Ubuntu and Apple's OS-X store LF only. Older Apple systems store CR only. This can cause problems when files produced by some programs are transferred between different types of computer. Fortunately, files created by Writer don't suffer from this problem.

Click *View > Nonprinting Characters*. You'll see apparent changes in your document. There's a small dot between most of the words. You'll see ➔ between words where you pressed TAB and you'll see a paragraph marker (¶) wherever you pressed RETURN.

When you click on Nonprinting Characters, Writer starts showing markers on the screen wherever it finds one of these special characters.

A common minor mistake is to unintentionally put more than one space between words when typing. With non-printing characters visible, you can spot extra dots where they shouldn't be and delete them.

You can also use Edit > Find & Replace to get rid of unwanted spaces, whether they're visible or not. Put the cursor in the Search for box and press the spacebar twice. Put the cursor in the Replace with box and press the spacebar once. You can now track down any unintentional sequences of two (or more) spaces and get rid of one of them by clicking [**Replace**].

Select the word *Barking* by double-clicking it. Place the mouse cursor over it and press and hold down the left mouse or trackpad button. While still holding the button down, move the cursor between ➜ and *Eating*. Release the button.

You see *BarkingEating*. You moved the highlighted word by **dragging and dropping** but it's not right. Press CTRL+Z to undo it.

Place the mouse cursor just before *Barking* and drag to just before *Sleeping*. *Barking* is now highlighted along with the ➜ after it: the word is selected along with the special TAB character. Retry dragging and dropping it to just before *Eating*. This time, it works properly: *Barking* and *Eating* are lined up with the tab marks on the ruler.

You can also copy selected text by dragging and dropping. Hold down the CTRL key before releasing the mouse button. The original selected text remains and a copy is dropped at the cursor position.

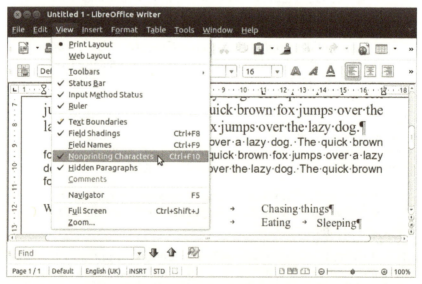

Click *View > Nonprinting Characters* again. The special markers are no longer shown. Try clicking several times. The markers appear and disappear. Leave them off.

The markers for non-printing characters won't appear when you print your document, even when they're visible on the screen.

Dragging and dropping and other editing such as replacing highlighted text or cutting and copying it to the clipboard works just the same when the special markers are not visible. If you want to include a space, tab or paragraph marker, you need to highlight the blank space on the screen where the marker would be.

Other non-printing characters are used to record changes in the text formatting such as different indents, justification, typefaces and text styles and sizes. Although they can't be made visible, they're also moved by cutting or copying and pasting or by dragging and dropping. The results of this aren't always what you'd expect or want. In particular, you should keep an eye on the text that was before and after something that you move to make sure that it doesn't change in an unexpected way.

What you learned:

- **What non-printing characters are.**
- **How to make non-printing characters visible on the screen.**
- **How to move or copy selected (highlighted) text by dragging and dropping.**
- **That you may need to include non printing characters when you move text around.**
- *That text formatting also uses non printing characters that you can't make visible.*
- *That these can cause problems when you move text.*
- *That different computers use incompatible ways of recording when RETURN is pressed.*
- *How to find and remove unintentional extra spaces between words.*

5.13 Checking your spelling

Try deliberately misspelling a word in the document, then move the text cursor elsewhere. Writer looks to see if the word is in its dictionary. When it can't find it, it puts a wavy red line under it. Move the mouse cursor over the offending word and right-click.

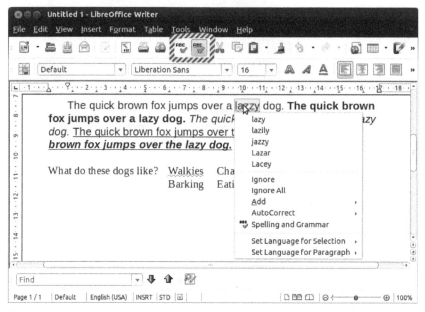

You see a list of possible replacements for the word. Click on the correct one. The word is replaced.

If you don't see the wavy red line, AutoSpellCheck may not be enabled. Click 🔤 (the right-most of the circled buttons) to enable it.

Clicking 🔤 again disables AutoSpellCheck if you find it annoying.

If the wavy line never appears, click Tools > Options. The Options dialogue box appears. Click the triangle to the left of Language Settings on the left hand side, then click Languages. Check that 🔤 appears alongside your language under Default languages for documents.

If 🔤 doesn't appear, the spellcheck dictionary is missing. Click ⬆ to the right of the language and choose a similar language where 🔤 does appear alongside. E.g. click on English (USA) in place of English (UK). Click OK . Of course, if you do this, the spellchecker will insist on slightly different spellings. Section 12.5 shows how to install the missing dictionary.

You'll notice that *Walkies* has a wavy red line. This is because it isn't in the dictionary but it doesn't mean that you must change the word. The wavy line won't appear when you print the document. If you want to, right-click the word and choose *Ignore* to ignore the word this time or *Ignore All* to ignore all instances of the word in the document. You can use *Add* to add the word to the dictionary so that it will be accepted in all your documents.

> *You can have multiple spell-check dictionaries installed, e.g. for different languages.*

> *Spell checkers can't spot cases where you've used a wrong sound-alike word that's also in the dictionary. E.g. "I ran this threw the spell chequer sew I know its write".*

If you click ᴬᴮᶜ✓ (the left-most of the circled buttons), Writer checks the whole document for misspelled words. When it finds one, it shows a dialogue box where you can make the same choices as above. This saves you from having to go through the whole document looking for wavy lines.

> *Microsoft Word includes a grammar checker which puts wavy green lines under suspect phrases or sentences, e.g. a sentence without a verb. This produces a lot of false alarms but can be useful. LibreOffice Writer also offers to check grammar but it needs a plug-in containing the rules for the particular language which may not be included in your installation.*

What you learned:

- **How to enable and disable spell checking as you type.**
- **What the wavy red lines mean and what to do about them.**
- **How to spell-check the whole document.**
- *What a spell-checker can't do.*
- *What a grammar checker does.*
- *That the grammar checker in LibreOffice Writer may not work.*

5.14 Saving the document

Click *File* > *Save*, press CTRL+S or click on 💾 (circled below).

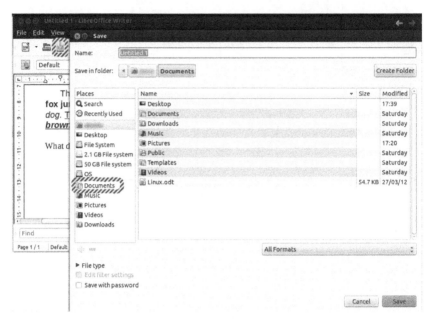

The *Save* dialogue box appears. The document doesn't have a name yet so *Untitled 1* is highlighted. You can just type a suitable name, e.g. *LazyDog*. Click *Documents* (circled). Press RETURN or click Save .

> *When a button is highlighted, you can press RETURN instead of clicking it.*
>
> *The document is copied from your computer's RAM to its hard disk. Now it's safely stored as a file even if the computer crashes or is turned off.*
>
> *LibreOffice should save documents in the Documents folder but there can be a bug causing it to save them elsewhere. Clicking Documents makes sure they are saved in the right place.*
>
> *You can choose a different folder if you want. Folders are explained in Chapter 6.*
>
> *LibreOffice normally automatically saves any changes you've made to a special file every 15 minutes or so. If LibreOffice or the computer crashes or there's a power failure, you'll be offered the chance to **recover** your document when you start Writer again. Some of your most recent changes may still be lost.*

Now that the document has a name, it shows this instead of *Untitled 1* on its titlebar. If you make more changes and save it again (by clicking ![save icon] or *File > Save* or pressing CTRL+S), the changed version immediately replaces the one on the hard disk without you being asked for its name. If you want to keep the old version and save the new version in a different folder and/or with a different name, you can click *File > Save As...* to open the *Save* dialogue box.

What you learned:

- **How to give your document a name and save it to the hard disk.**

- **How to save the document again after you've made changes to it.**

- **How to save a new version of the document with a different name.**

- *That you can press RETURN instead of clicking on a highlighted button.*

- *That you can recover most of your document after a crash.*

5.15 Printing the document

Things can sometimes go wrong when you try to print a document. You already saved it – it won't be lost even if the computer locks up or crashes.

Click *File > Print....* A dialogue box opens

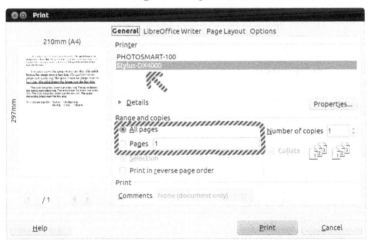

You might have more than one printer set up on your computer. Make sure that the right one is highlighted (as arrowed): if it isn't, click on the name of the printer you want to use. Make sure that the printer is switched on and isn't out of paper.

> *If you only see Generic Printer or you don't see the printer you want, it may not be set up on your computer. See Section 12.7.*

You want to print the whole of your document. If the radio button to the left of *All pages* (circled) isn't filled in as shown here, click on it.

> *If you have a long document and don't want to print all of it, click on the radio button to the left of Pages (circled). Type the page numbers you want to print in the box to the right of Pages.*

> *The page numbers should be typed with commas between them. You can also specify ranges of pages by putting dashes between them. E.g. 1,3,5-7,10- will print pages 1, 3, 5, 6, 7 and page 10 onwards.*

> *You'll notice that the dialogue box lets you print several copies at once and choose whether to have them collated. If you choose not to* **collate***, the printer prints all copies of each page together. They will print faster (especially if the pages include graphics) but you'll need to put them in order by hand afterwards.*

Click [**Print**]. The document is printed – perhaps after a short delay.

> *One of your printers will be set as the default. If you want to print the whole document to it, you can click 🖨 on the toolbar instead of using File > Print.... When you move the mouse cursor over the 🖨 button, the tooltip shows which printer would be used.*

Click (x) to close Writer.

> *If you forget to save the file or if you've made changes since it was last saved, you'll be asked whether you want to save or discard your changes.*

What you learned:

- **How to print a document.**
- **How to select the printer you want to use and the pages you want to print.**
- *That it's wise to save your document before you try to print it.*
- *How to choose which pages and how many copies to print.*

- *What collation is and when you might not want to use it.*

- *How to print the whole document with a single click.*

- *That Writer will try to make sure that you save your document before closing the program.*

5.16 Documents attached to an e-mail

You can send a file to someone else by **attaching** it to an e-mail. This book doesn't attempt to describe how to send and receive e-mails. There are too many different e-mail systems.

However, there's an important thing you need to know.

When you click on a document on a web page or attached to an e-mail, a copy is put in a special temporary folder on the hard disk and your word processor is started and told to open it.

With Ubuntu, Writer knows that the document is in a temporary folder and prevents you from making any changes until you've saved it in a safe permanent location.

> *If you're swearing at your computer because it won't let you edit a document, this could be the reason.*

When you're using Windows, things may be different. *Word 2010* on *Windows 7* is OK but some other combinations of word processor and Windows are happy to let you work all day on the document, then click *Save*. What you don't realise is that the version with all your changes was written back to the temporary folder. Windows may decide at any time that it's not needed any more and delete it. Even if the file isn't deleted, it's often impossible to find out where it's hidden.

> *Many people I know have lost hours of work because of this.*

Make it a habit to always click *File > Save as...* and choose a folder such as *Documents* before you start work on any document that you opened directly from an e-mail or web page.

6 Files and folders

This chapter explains how documents, etc. are stored on your computer's hard disk and how to access, organise and move them.

6.1 The hard disk

In the Launcher, click 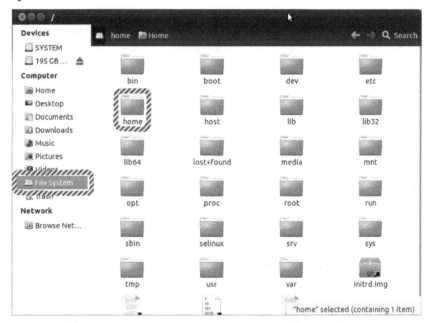. The **Nautilus** file manager opens. Click ⚹ File System (circled below). This takes you to the **root** of the **file system** on the hard disk.

You see icons looking like **folders** in a filing cabinet. Double click the one marked *home* (circled but it might be in a different place). It opens.

> *Each folder has a name and it can contain files. A file is like a length of paper tape punched with the bytes that make up the document or program. Imagine that a name is written on it and it's stored in a folder in a filing cabinet.*
>
> *A folder can contain other folders – this would be useful in a real filing cabinet too but it would be physically hard to achieve.*

You can't have two files or folders with the same name in the same folder because the computer would be as confused as you'd be.

A folder may also be called a **directory**: they're the same thing.

Along with home, you'll have noticed many other folders in the screenshot above. These contain files used by the Linux operating system. You normally shouldn't mess with these folders and files but it can be useful to know what some of the folders contain.

- The bin, lib, sbin and usr folders contain programs, e.g. LibreOffice.

- The etc folder contains many operating system settings, e.g. the list of users and their encrypted passwords.

- The host folder contains the Windows C: files: it's only present with a WUBI installation.

- The media and mnt folders contain mounted disk drives (Section 6.4).

- The var folder contains system data which changes a lot, e.g. log files and e-mail queues.

You see a folder with your user name. Double click to open it.

If there are other users with Ubuntu accounts on the computer, you'll see folders with their names too. See Section 12.9.

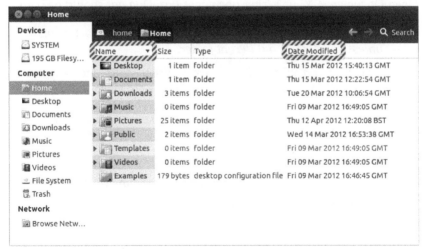

You see icons or a list of your personal files and folders. Click *View >
List*. This makes sure that the files and folders are shown in a list with
Size and *Date Modified* as shown above. You'll see folders called
Desktop and *Documents*.

> *Unlike LibreOffice, Nautilus works as it supposed to: you need
> to move the mouse cursor to the top of the screen to see its menu
> names (e.g. View).*

> *If there are a lot of files and folders in the list, a scroll bar will
> appear to its right. The Nautilus scroll bar is a new Unity
> design: it saves space by being much narrower than the Firefox
> and LibreOffice ones. When you move the mouse cursor over it
> (on the right-hand side of the window), a button appears that
> you can drag up and down.*

If you click on *Name* (circled), the files and folders are sorted alphabetically. The triangle next to *Name* and the shading of the file and folder
names shows that this is the order. Click on *Name* again. The triangle
flips over and the sorting order is reversed.

Click on *Date Modified* (circled). The triangle appears next to this and
the files and folders are sorted by the date and time that the last change
to them was made. This is very useful if you can't remember the name
of a file that you need to find but you know approximately when it was
created or changed.

> *You can sort on any of the other columns instead. Just click on
> the column title.*

Open *Documents*. Your Writer document *LazyDog.odt* should be there.

> *When you save a new file, LibreOffice saves it in Documents
> unless you choose a different folder.*

Double click on *LazyDog.odt*. It opens: Writer starts and displays it.
You aren't going to do anything with it. Click ⊗ to close it.

> *Section 12.3 shows how you can open files and folders with a
> single click.*

What you learned:

- **What the Nautilus file manager is and how to start it.**
- **What folders and files are.**
- **That they have icons and names.**
- **How to open a folder or a file such as a document.**

- That you have a personal folder in *home* with a *Desktop* and a *Documents* folder in it.

- That you can list the contents of a folder in various orders including by name or by date modified – this helps when you're looking for a file.

- That Writer saved the *LazyDog* document in your *Documents* folder.

- That you can start with the file system root and work your way to any file on the computer.

- *That a folder and a directory are the same thing.*

- *That programs and settings are kept as files in folders that you normally leave alone.*

- *That the Nautilus Unity scroll bar is a bit different.*

6.2 Making folders and moving files

Click *File > Create New Folder*. A folder appears with the name *Untitled Folder* highlighted. Type *WP files* and press RETURN.

You just made a brand new folder. Its name was set to *Untitled Folder* but, because it was highlighted, anything you typed replaced the name and it's now called *WP files*.

> *You can change the name of an existing folder or file by right-clicking on it and clicking Rename....*

Put the mouse cursor over *LazyDog.odt* and right-click. A list appears. Click *Cut*. The file is moved to the clipboard. Open the new *WP files* folder. Of course it's empty - you only just made it. Right-click on the empty list and click on *Paste*. *LazyDog.odt* is moved to the *WP files* folder.

> *Of course, if you'd clicked Copy instead of Cut, the original LazyDog.odt would have been left in Documents and a new copy would have been put in WP files.*

> *You can cut, copy and paste folders as well as files and you can also use the Nautilus Edit menu or the usual keyboard shortcuts (CTRL+X, CTRL+C and CTRL+V).*

What you learned:

- How to make and name a new folder.

- **How to move a file to a different folder by cutting and pasting.**
- **That you can cut, copy or paste a file or folder by right-clicking.**
- *How to rename a file or folder.*
- *How to paste a copy of a file in a different folder.*

6.3 The clipboard

You've used the clipboard to copy text and paste it somewhere else in a document and to cut or copy a file and paste it in a different folder.

The clipboard is part of Ubuntu and every program can use it, including Writer. As well as files, folders and text, it can hold other things such as pictures and spreadsheets as you'll see in Chapter 10. Because it's part of Ubuntu, it can be used to move something from one program to another although only if the program you're pasting it into knows what to do with it.

For example, if you're looking at a web page using Firefox, you can select text or even a picture on the page, copy it and paste it into your Writer document. If you have two documents open at once, you can cut or copy text from one document and paste it into the other one.

The clipboard only holds one thing at a time. When you copy something to it, it replaces whatever was there before. Unlike text in a Writer document, if you cut a file or folder to the clipboard then replace it with something else before pasting, the file or folder isn't deleted. It's left where it was.

6.4 Using a thumbdrive

If you have a USB thumbdrive / Data Stick, plug it into any USB port on your computer. If in doubt, look at the rectangular metal connector on the thumbdrive, then look for a socket on the front or side of your computer that's the same size and shape.

USB (Universal Serial Bus) is a way to connect various devices to the computer including thumbdrives, external hard disks, printers and scanners. Music players, cameras and mobile phones can be connected with USB so you can copy files to and from them.

Wait a few seconds. Nautilus may open showing the folders and files saved on the thumbdrive (there may not be any). You can click its ⊗ to close it.

Click ▢ on the Launcher to see your previous Nautilus window (or open a new one). An item is listed under *Devices* with an icon that looks like a thumbdrive (circled below). Click on it. You see folders and files on the thumbdrive (if there are any) – the computer views it as a disk drive.

Click ▣ if needed to maximise the window. Click *View > Extra Pane*. You see the folders and files listed twice in separate panes of the window.

Under the list of devices on the left side is a list of useful folders on your computer. Click on *Documents* (circled below). One of the two panes changes to show the files and folders in your *Documents* folder. The *WP files* folder is there.

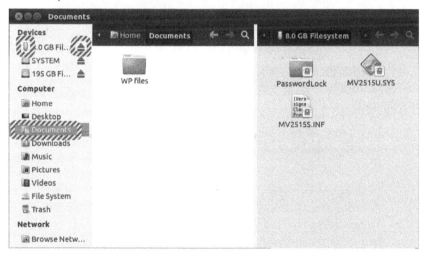

Double click on *WP files* to open it. *LazyDog.odt* is there. Place the mouse cursor over it and hold down the left mouse button. Drag *Lazy-Dog.odt* to a blank area in the other pane. You'll notice that a small + sign appears.

Release the mouse button. *LazyDog.odt* is copied to the thumbdrive.

If you'd dragged LazyDog.odt over an existing folder on the thumbdrive, the copy would have been put in that folder.

Ubuntu left the file in WP files and made a copy because you dragged it from there (on the hard disk) to a different disk.

You can use the two panes to see files in different folders on your hard disk too. If you drag files or folders between the two panes, they'll be moved rather than copied. You can make a copy instead by holding down CTRL before releasing the button.

If you can see both the destination folder and the file or folder you want to copy or move, you can drag it in a single pane.

Open *LazyDog* on the thumbdrive. Writer starts and displays your document. You aren't going to do anything with it and you can close it.

If you wanted, you could make changes to the document but, when they're saved, this will be on the thumbdrive and the copy on the hard disk remains as it was. This soon gets confusing. There's a risk of ending up with two different copies of the document where some changes are in one and some are in the other.

Click *View > Extra Pane* again. One of the two panes disappears.

The two panes are extremely useful when you need to compare files and their modification dates in two different places.

Look for the thumbdrive where it's listed under *Devices*. ⏏ (circled above) shows to the right of the drive under *Devices*, showing that it is mounted.

If you're used to Windows, you'll know that it uses letters to identify disk drives. For example, the hard disk is usually Drive C.

Unix-based systems such as Ubuntu use a different method. Additional disk drives are **mounted** *so that they appear as folders within the existing file system, usually inside the media or mnt folders mentioned in Section 6.1.*

Click ⏏. Perhaps after a short delay, ⏏ disappears. The thumbdrive is **unmounted** and you can safely unplug it.

Saving changes on the thumbdrive can take some time. If you unplug it while ⏏ *is still showing there's a risk of losing files on it.*

If you plug the thumbdrive into a different computer (perhaps a Windows one), you can copy files from the thumbdrive to its hard drive. You may not be able to open the files unless the computer has the same programs installed on it. Again of course you must be sure that any changes you make are to the newest version of the document.

You can copy a document file such as LazyDog to a thumbdrive or removable disk and give it to someone or you can attach it to an e-mail and send it to them.

What you learned:

- **How to plug in and safely unplug the thumbdrive**
- **That the computer sees it as another disk drive, even though there's no spinning disk.**
- **How to see two the contents of two folders or drives at once.**
- **That you can go directly to a folder listed on the left hand side by clicking on it.**
- **How to copy a file to the thumbdrive by dragging and dropping.**
- **How to use the thumbdrive to copy a file onto another computer.**
- *That you can move a file to a different folder on the same disk by dragging and dropping.*
- *That holding down CTRL copies the file instead of moving it.*
- *How, instead of using drive letters, Ubuntu mounts disks in different folders in the file system.*
- *That you can open and edit a document directly from the thumbdrive but this may not be a good idea.*

6.5 Your Windows files

The folder you're currently in and the folders containing it are listed at the top (circled). You can go to any of them by clicking its name. Click on *Documents*. You're back in the *Documents* folder.

If you also have Windows on your computer, you might see one or more disk drives listed under *Devices* (circled above).

One of these drives may contain your Windows files. The name of this drive may vary. Click on these disk drives in turn. When you see a *Windows* folder and either a *Documents and Settings* (Windows XP) or a *Users* (Vista/Windows 7) folder, you've found it.

> *You're probably using WUBI. If so, click* ⚏ File System *(as in Section 6.1) then open the host folder to see your Windows files.*

Open *Documents and Settings* or *Users*. Open the folder that appears with your Windows user name.

> *Unfortunately, your Windows account and user name may not be the same. You might have to try a couple of different folders.*

If you have Windows XP, open *My Documents*. If you have Vista or Windows 7, open *Documents*. You see your Windows Documents files and folders.

> *As you can see, it's quite easy to get to your Windows files from Ubuntu. Unfortunately, it isn't possible to get to your Ubuntu*

files from Windows unless you install a special, hard to find program.

If you think you'll want to use a file in Windows, you can copy or move it to your Windows Documents folder before shutting down Ubuntu. If you make changes to it in Windows, be sure to use the new version after you switch back to Ubuntu.

What you learned:

- **How to go to a folder containing the one you're currently viewing.**
- **Where to find your Windows document files.**
- *That you can't see your Ubuntu files from Windows.*
- *That you can copy or move files from Ubuntu before switching to Windows.*

6.6 Selecting, deleting and linking

Click *Documents* on the left side of the Nautilus window and open *WP files*. Right-click *LazyDog.odt* and click *Make Link* in the list that appears.

Link to LazyDog.odt appears. Place the mouse cursor below and to its right. Hold down the left mouse button and drag upwards and to the left. A shaded rectangular **marquee** appears. Keep dragging until it covers both *Link to LazyDog.odt* and *LazyDog.odt* itself.

Release the mouse button. Both files are selected and highlighted. Press DELETE. The files disappear.

Oops. We didn't really want to delete them. Don't panic, we can get them back. Click 🗑 Trash below the list of folders on the left side. The deleted files appear.

There might be a lot of other deleted files too and some of them might have the same names. Click View > List. The files are now in a list with additional details including their original locations.

Click the Trashed On heading. The files are sorted by deletion date and time. It's easy to see the two that we want.

You can also open the Trash folder by clicking 🗑 *on the Launcher.*

Click on one of the files. Hold down CTRL and click on the other. Both files are selected and highlighted.

> *You can select multiple files and/or folders using CTRL+A, by dragging the mouse cursor over them, by selecting them individually while holding down CTRL or by selecting the first one, then holding down SHIFT and selecting the last one in a list. Once you've selected them, you can copy or move them all at once.*

Right click on either of the highlighted files and click *Restore* in the list that appears.

> *When you delete a file, Nautilus usually just moves it to the Trash folder in case you need to restore it. If your hard disk gets full, Ubuntu starts deleting files in the Trash folder. Don't rely on them being there for long.*

> *You can get rid of embarrassing files in the Trash folder by right-clicking and clicking on Delete Permanently. You can also permanently delete any file by holding down SHIFT when you press DELETE.*

> *When a file is permanently deleted, its space on the disk is marked as unused but the file data isn't destroyed until something else is written there. There are still ways to recover the deleted file. If you need it to be gone forever, you can use* **shred** *to overwrite it (Section 12.11).*

Click *Documents* on the left side of the Nautilus window and open *WP files* again. The two files have reappeared.

Drag *Link to LazyDog.odt* over the *Desktop* folder on the left hand side and drop it there.

> *You can drag and drop files and folders onto any of the folders listed on the left hand side.*

Minimise Nautilus. You now see *Link to LazyDog.odt* on the desktop. Double click it. Writer starts and opens it. Click ⊗ to close it.

> *Desktop is a special folder – anything it in appears on the computer desktop.*

> *A* **link** *is a pointer to another file or folder. Its icon includes a little arrow. When a document has a link on the desktop, it's very easy to open it.*

You can put a link in any folder, not just on the desktop. When you click to open a link, Ubuntu finds the file or folder that it points to and opens that instead.

As well as links, you can put documents and folders themselves on the Desktop. Section 6.7 explains why this often isn't a good idea.

You can get rid of a link by selecting it and pressing DELETE: the file or folder that it points to isn't affected. But be sure it's a link (with the little arrow): the file or folder itself might be on the desktop.

Click ▦ on the Launcher to restore the Nautilus window. *Documents* should still be one of the containing folders listed across the top.

Right click on it and click *Properties* in the list that appears. A dialogue box opens. Click on the *Basic* tab. The number and total size of all the files and folders in *Documents* is shown beside *Contents:*. This will be useful information when you make a backup copy. Click [Close] or ⊗ to close the dialogue box.

You'll want to make folders in Documents and organise your documents in them. It's up to you how to set up the folders: it's like planning a filing cabinet although a bit more flexible. You can get to any of the folders from Documents so you'll only want to put links on the desktop for the files and folders that you use most often. If you put too many links there, it gets messy and confusing.

What you learned:

- **How to create a link (shortcut) to a file or folder.**
- **How to select multiple files or folders by dragging.**
- **How to delete selected files and folders.**
- **How to add a file or folder to a selection by pressing CTRL.**
- **How to restore a file or folder that you deleted accidentally.**
- **How to put and use a link on the desktop.**
- **How to move a file to a different folder on the same hard disk by dragging and dropping or by cutting and pasting.**
- **How to get quickly to a folder or open a document by putting a link on the desktop.**
- **How to see the total size of all the files in a folder.**

- *How to select and copy, move or delete multiple files or folders.*

- *How to permanently delete or shred a file.*

- *That the desktop displays files, folders and shortcuts placed in the special Desktop folder.*

- *How to identify and delete a link.*

- *That this doesn't delete the file it points to.*

6.7 Making backups

If the hard disk in your computer fails or if the computer breaks down or is lost or stolen, you could lose all your files. These could include not only documents that you've worked on for weeks but also irreplaceable files such as your photos.

Your personal document files are usually all in *Documents*. You can drag or copy and paste *Documents* to a thumbdrive. Safely remove the thumbdrive and store it away from the computer.

> *You could have dragged WP files itself to the Desktop folder instead of leaving it in Documents and putting a shortcut on the desktop. That's easier to do but its files wouldn't be backed up when you make a copy of Documents.*

If there's enough space on the thumbdrive, you can update the backup by renaming the old *Documents* folder on it, copying the new version to it, then deleting the old version. If there isn't enough space to do this, you'll have to delete the old version before copying the new version. That's a bit riskier. Make absolutely sure you're deleting the backup *Documents* and not *Documents* on the computer itself!

You might have music, photos and videos in your *Music*, *Pictures* and *Videos* folders. You can copy these folders too. However, they tend to take much more space than your documents and the copies may not fit on the thumbdrive. You can buy an external hard disk instead. It works exactly the same way as the thumbdrive but holds much more data.

You can use two external disks or thumbdrives so that one is always stored safely, even when you're updating files on the other one. Ideally, keep one of them in a different building in case of burglary or fire.

> *There are two different types of external hard disks available: ones that are powered from the computer and ones that have a separate power supply that needs to be plugged in. The ones*

with a separate power supply are generally less expensive but also less convenient.

If you use two thumbdrives or external disks and check once in a while that they're both working reliably, you can keep your documents and photos safe forever. They won't fade, crumble or get thrown away.

Ubuntu includes a specialised backup program which can save time because it only copies new and changed files to the backup.

There are services available that back up your files to a server on the internet. They solve the problem of keeping the backup in a different building. However, if you have confidential information, are you sure no-one is going to snoop in the backup copy?

What you learned:

- **What a backup is and why it's important to make one.**
- **That all that's normally needed is to make a copy of *Documents* on a thumbdrive.**
- **That you can use an external hard disk instead of a thumbdrive – it holds more.**
- **That it's a good idea to keep two backups and have one of them in a different building.**
- *Why you should try to keep all your documents in the Documents folder.*
- *That music, pictures and videos are kept in other folders that you may need to back up too.*
- *That computer files and photos can outlast paper.*
- *That there are special programs for making backups which may be faster.*
- *That you can save your backups over the internet.*

7 Structuring a document

This chapter covers LibreOffice Writer features that make it easier to type a document, format it consistently, give it a structure such as sections or chapters and add headers and footers and a table of contents. It covers additional features such as bullet points and numbered lists and discusses templates and saving documents using different file formats, e.g. so that they can be opened with Microsoft Word.

By now, you should be quite familiar with drop down menus, dialogue boxes, etc. You won't need such detailed instructions and so many screenshots.

7.1 Autocompletion and autocorrection

You need to make a new document containing some extracts from this book. Start Writer as in Section 5.1 and type the following into the new document (press RETURN when you see ¶ and don't worry at all about formatting at this stage):

Introduction¶
Are you just starting with a computer to write letters?¶
Have you been using a word processor for some time but still find it intimidating

You'll probably see an odd thing as you type *intimidating*: something like int*roduction* appears. This is a feature called **autocompletion** or **Word Completion**. Writer saw that you already typed the word *Introduction* and it thinks you might be typing it again. If it was the word you wanted, you could press RETURN once you'd typed *int* and the word would be completed automatically. You can try it now if you want.

It's not the word you want though so, if you did press RETURN, you need to delete it (or at least the wrong bit of it). Start typing again, ignoring any highlighted word completion text that pops up:

intimidating and feel that you don't understand what it's doing?¶
If you fit either description, this book is meant for you.¶
¶
Behind the screen¶

"I'm buying a new computer. It has:¶
An Int

Word completion kicks in again but you might be typing *Introduction* or *Intimidating*. Writer shows one of them but you can choose the other with CTRL+TAB. If the word you want appears, you can press RETURN.

Alternatively, you could type another letter. If you typed *r*, only *Intro-duction* would fit. If you typed *i* instead, only *Intimidating* would fit. Type *e*. Nothing matches and the highlighted word completion text disappears. The word you want is *Intel* so type *l* and a space.

> *Sometimes you need to press RETURN to start a new line or paragraph while word completion text is showing. Press the ESC (Escape) key at the top left of the keyboard to clear the completion text, then press RETURN.*

> *If you decide word completion is more trouble than it's worth, click Tools > AutoCorrect Options.... A dialogue box appears. Click on the Word Completion tab, clear the tick-box next to Enable word completion and click OK .*

Writer also has an **auto-correction** feature. For example, if you type space, *i* and space, it automatically changes *i* to *I*. It also automatically capitalises the first word of anything it thinks is a new sentence. Sometimes it makes changes that you don't want. Just go back and undo the change it made – it'll get the hint.

Continue typing the rest of the document:

> *Dual Core processor¶*
> *4GB (232 bytes) of RAM"¶*
> *Chapters 2-6 of this book are general.¶*
> *¶*
> *Basics of Ubuntu¶*
> *This chapter covers basics such as starting and closing programs.¶*
> *Type your password and press RETURN.¶*
> *Clicking with the mouse¶*
> *Instead of using the left button, you can click with the right hand one. This has a different effect from normal clicking.¶*
> *It's possible to change settings so the mouse buttons are switched.¶*
> *Starting the Web Browser¶*
> *Click the Firefox icon on the Launcher.¶*
> *The web browser starts.¶*

What you learned:

- **What word completion is and how to use it.**
- **That you can usually ignore it and just carry on typing.**
- **How to choose from several possible words.**
- *How to suppress word completion so you can press RETURN.*
- *How to turn word completion off.*
- *What auto-correction is and how to override it.*

7.2 Formatting individual characters

The text you typed in shows what 4GB is as a power of two but it needs to be formatted to make sense. Drag to select the second and third digits in *232*. Click *Format > Character....* A dialogue box appears. Click on the *Position* tab. There are three radio buttons marked *Superscript, Normal* and *Subscript*. Select the one marked *Superscript* and click OK . The line now reads *4GB (2^{32} bytes) of RAM"* which is correct.

You can also subscript characters, e.g. H_2O. The tabs in the dialogue box let you change other things including the colour of text and different styles of underlining. You see a preview of the selected text as you make changes. Explore the various options.

The document should now read:

Introduction
Are you just starting with a computer to write letters?
Have you been using a word processor for some time but still find it intimidating and feel that you don't understand what it's doing?
If you fit either description, this book is meant for you.

Behind the screen
"I'm buying a new computer. It has:
An Intel Dual Core processor
4GB (2^{32} bytes) of RAM"
Chapters 2-6 of this book are general.

Basics of Ubuntu.
This chapter covers basics such as starting and closing programs.
Type your password and press RETURN.
Clicking with the mouse
Instead of using the left button, you can click with the right hand one. This has a different effect from normal clicking.

It's possible to change settings so the mouse buttons are switched.
Starting the Web Browser
Click the Firefox icon on the Launcher.
The web browser starts.

What you learned:

- **How to create a superscripted character.**

- *How to subscript a character.*

- *How to change the colour of characters, etc.*

7.3 Numbering and bullets

Highlight part or all of the two paragraphs following *Introduction*. Remember that a new paragraph started when you pressed RETURN.

To the right of the four buttons on the toolbar for text justification are buttons to turn numbering or bullets on and off. Tooltips help you to find them.

Click on the numbering button (:≡). The lines become automatically numbered:

1. *Are you just starting with a computer to write letters?*

2. *Have you been using a word processor for some time but still find it intimidating and feel that you don't understand what it's doing?*

*A **toolbar** appears below the document containing additional buttons which let you adjust the numbering. For example, put the cursor in the paragraph numbered 2. and click ➡. The paragraph is demoted to sub-paragraph 1 of paragraph 1. Click ⬅ (or use CTRL+Z) to promote it back as paragraph 2.*

When you have several levels of numbered sub-paragraphs, you can use ⬅ and ➡ to promote and demote individual paragraphs. ⬅ and ➡ promote or demote a paragraph along with all of its sub-paragraphs

Clicking ⌗ at the right-hand end of the toolbar opens a tabbed dialogue box where, among other things, you can change the numbering type, e.g. to a, b, c or to Roman numerals. You can experiment with the other buttons in the toolbar – they have tool-tips

With the two paragraphs still selected, click ⊞ repeatedly. The numbers appear and disappear. Leave them on.

Place the text cursor just after *doing?* and press RETURN:

1. *Are you just starting with a computer to write letters?*

2. *Have you been using a word processor for some time but still find it intimidating and feel that you don't understand what it's doing?*

3.

A number appears and you could start typing a new numbered paragraph. Press BACKSPACE once. The number disappears and you could start typing an additional paragraph following on from paragraph 2.

> *Sometimes you need more than one paragraph under the same number.*

Press BACKSPACE again. The numbered list is ended and you can start typing a normal paragraph.

Press BACKSPACE a third time. It's now as if you never pressed RETURN. Select the two paragraphs again and click on the bullets button (⊞). The numbers change to dots (**bullets**):

• *Are you just starting with a computer to write letters?*

• *Have you been using a word processor for some time but still find it intimidating and feel that you don't understand what it's doing?*

Bullets work much the same as numbers and have a similar toolbar.

What you learned:

• **How to create a list of numbered or lettered items.**

• **How to add an item to the list.**

• **How to start a new line in an existing list item without it becoming a new list item.**

• **What a bullet is and how to create a list with them.**

• **How to end the list.**

• ***How to create and modify a multi-level list (e.g. 1, 1.1, 1.2, 2, 3).***

- *How to change the numbering style, e.g. to Roman numerals.*

7.4 Formatting paragraphs

To the left of the typeface selector box (saying e.g. *Liberation Serif)* is the **paragraph style selector box**. Click on ▨ to the left of that. The floating *Styles and Formatting* window appears. Make sure ▨ (for paragraph styles) at the top is highlighted.

At the bottom of the window, you can choose which paragraph styles are visible. Click on ▨. A drop-down list appears. Click on *Text Styles*.

Click anywhere in your document and press CTRL+A to select all the text.

Double-click on *Text body* in the *Styles and Formatting* window. Your document is reformatted with blank space between every paragraph.

At the bottom of the *Styles and Formatting* window, choose *Chapter Styles* instead of *Text Styles*. Two styles (*Subtitle* and *Title*) are now shown in the window.

In the document, position the cursor anywhere in the first line (*Intro-duction*), click to deselect other paragraphs and double-click *Title* in the *Styles and Formatting* window. The whole line is given a different paragraph style supposed to be suitable for a chapter title. Its typeface, style and size changes and it becomes centred.

Position the cursor in the line that reads *Clicking with the mouse*. Double-click *Subtitle* in the *Styles and Formatting* window. The line is given a style supposed to be suitable for a subsection of a chapter. Repeat this with the line that reads *Starting the Web browser*.

Close the *Styles and Formatting* window by clicking its ⊗.

Position the cursor on the blank line above *Basics of Ubuntu* and press DELETE.

> *We put a blank line to make it easier to spot the new chapter. It won't be needed any more.*

Make sure the cursor is on *Basics of Ubuntu*. Choose *Title* from the paragraph style selector box (to the right of ▨). The line changes to a chapter title like *Introduction*.

> *The paragraph style selector box includes all styles already used anywhere in your document. You can use it to apply them to other paragraphs without having to open the Styles and*

Formatting window. Of course, when the window is open, you can double-click the style there instead.

What you learned:

- **How to change all paragraphs in a document to the Writer preset** *Text body* **style**

- **How to change individual paragraphs such as chapter titles to a different preset style.**

- **That you can select a paragraph style using either the Styles and Formatting window or the Style Selector box.**

7.5 Modifying paragraph styles

Writer's preset chapter styles leave something to be desired. Click ▦ to open the *Styles and Formatting* window again and make sure that *Chapter Styles* are selected. Right-click on *Subtitle* and click on *Modify....* A dialogue box appears. Click on the *Organizer* tab and click on the *AutoUpdate* box so that it's ticked. Click on the *Outline and Numbering tab.* Set *Outline level* to *Level 2* and check that *Numbering style* is *None.* Click ▭ OK ▭.

Put the text cursor in the line *Starting the Web browser.* Click ▤ to left-justify it. The change is made automatically to all paragraphs with the *Subtitle* style – in this case *Clicking with the mouse* changes too.

This happened because you ticked AutoUpdate.

When you set a paragraph to use a particular style, this doesn't prevent you from making other changes to the style of individual characters or words or even making changes to the style of the whole paragraph, e.g. by changing its justification or by clicking Format > Paragraph... and making other changes in the dialogue box. Unless the assigned style has AutoUpdate ticked, the changes won't affect other paragraphs using the same style.

This can cause problems: a paragraph may look odd or behave strangely in the table of contents because of some local formatting that you've forgotten about. You can remove all local formatting of a paragraph by selecting Clear formatting in the paragraph style selector box, then setting the required paragraph style again.

You'll often want to make tweaks to individual paragraphs of body text. It wouldn't be a good idea to tick AutoUpdate for the Text body style.

Right-click on *Title* in the *Styles and Formatting* window and click on *Modify...*. Click on the *Text Flow* tab in the dialogue box. Look for the *Breaks* section and tick the box next to *Insert*. Make sure the boxes to the right read *Page* and *Before*. This will make every paragraph formatted as *Title* start on a new page.

Click on the *Outline and Numbering* tab. Set *Outline level* to *Level 1* and *Numbering style* to *Numbering 1* (you may need to scroll down to see it). Click [OK].

Each chapter now starts on a new page and its title shows the chapter number.

Oops, we missed a chapter!

Position the cursor on the blank line above *Behind the screen* and press DELETE. Make sure the cursor is on *Behind the screen*. Choose *Title* from the paragraph style selector box.

The line becomes the title for Chapter 2. *Basics of Windows* is automatically renumbered as Chapter 3.

When you right-click on a paragraph style in the Styles and Formatting box, New... is another option. If you click on this, a copy of the style is made. You give the copy a new name and can change any other settings you want to create a custom style.

There's a Next Style option on the Organizer tab which says what style is automatically given to the next paragraph when you finish a paragraph in your new style and press RETURN. If the new style is intended for some type of body text, you'll usually want to use the same style in the next paragraph too. If it's intended for a heading or caption, you'll usually be using Text body as the next style.

When you right-click on one of your custom styles in Styles and Formatting, you'll see an option to delete it. Although you can modify the Writer predefined styles, you can't rename or delete them.

Styles that you add and changes that you make to predefined styles are saved with your document and reloaded when you open it but they don't affect other documents. When you start a new document, the styles available are the original ones.

What you learned:

- **How to adjust and improve the Writer preset paragraph styles.**

- **That a change to a paragraph style immediately affects all the paragraphs of that style in the document. You don't have to find them all and change them one by one.**

- **That paragraphs of a particular style (e.g. chapter titles) can be automatically numbered.**

- **That the numbers update automatically when you make changes to the document.**

- *What AutoUpdate does and when to avoid using it.*

- *That you can still change the formatting of text and individual paragraphs.*

- *How to remove any formatting of an individual paragraph.*

- *How to create and delete custom paragraph styles.*

- *That changes to paragraph styles only affect the current document.*

7.6 Using multi-level numbering

This is a more powerful way to number chapters and chapter sections.

Right-click *Title* in the *Styles and Formatting* box and click *Modify....* On the *Outline & Numbering* tab, set *Numbering Style* to *None* (you may need to scroll up to see this choice). Click OK . The chapters are no longer numbered.

You may have problems if you try to use two methods of numbering at the same time.

You can close the *Styles and Formatting* window by clicking its ⊗.

Click *Tools > Outline Numbering....* A dialogue box opens. Click on the *Numbering* tab.

At the left hand side is a box titled *Level* containing the numbers *1* to *10*. Click on *1*. Set *Paragraph Style* to *Title* and *Number* to *1, 2, 3, ...* Click in the *After* box and press SPACEBAR.

LibreOffice should automatically add a space after the chapter number in the Table of Contents you'll make later on but it doesn't.

Click on *2* in the *Level* box. Set *Paragraph Style* to *Subtitle, Number* to *1, 2, 3, ...* and *Show sublevels* to *2*. Click in the *After* box and press SPACEBAR. Click OK .

You see that the chapters are numbered 1-3 as before but the two Subtitle paragraphs in Chapter 3 are now numbered 3.1 and 3.2.

What you've done is to tell Writer that paragraphs set to the Title style (chapter titles) are the highest numbering level (1) and to show their numbers. Paragraphs set to the Subtitle style are the next numbering level (2). Because you set Show sublevels to 2, they show not only their own numbers but the number of the chapter as well. This can be useful if you want to refer to them elsewhere in the document.

If you try to modify the Title or Subtitle styles, you'll now find that most options on the Outline and Numbering tab are shown in grey (greyed out) and you can't change them. In this case, it's because the styles are selected in Tools > Outline Numbering. Unfortunately it's often hard to know why icons, menu items or options in a dialogue box are greyed out.

What you learned:

- **How to apply an overall numbering scheme to your document.**

- *That icons, menu items or options in a dialogue box are sometimes greyed out and cannot be used or changed.*

- *That it may not be easy to figure out why an icon, menu item or option is greyed out.*

7.7 Inserting a table

In Section 5.7 you saw how tab stops can be used to line up text in columns. You could use this to type a table in your document but Writer has an easier and more powerful way.

Click at the end of the last line in Chapter 1 (*If you fit either description, this book is meant for you.*) and press RETURN.

Click *Table > Insert > Table....* A dialogue box opens. Set *Columns* to *4*. Tick the *Heading* box. Click OK . A blank table is created with the cursor in the top left rectangle.

Type *Program* and press TAB. The cursor moves to the next box. Type *Formatting* and press TAB. Type *Styles* in the next box and *Grammar* in the last (top right) box. After you press TAB, the cursor should be in the left hand box on the second row. Type *Gedit* and press TAB.

> *When you're typing in a table, TAB moves to the next box to the right.*

> *Because you ticked the Heading box when you inserted the table, the first row is formatted differently from the others. The Repeat heading box was also ticked so, if the table won't all fit on one page, the first row will be repeated above any rows that end up on a new page.*

> *If you'd ticked Don't split table, Writer would start the table on a new page if it wouldn't all fit on the current one.*

Type *No, No* and *No* in the three boxes to the right of *Gedit*, pressing TAB after each *No*. A new blank row appears.

Type *Libreoffice, Yes, Yes* and *No* in the four boxes in the new row.

Type *Microsoft Word, Yes, Yes* and *Yes* in the four boxes of the next row.

Oops, two problems! You've got another blank row and you should have capitalised the *O* in *LibreOffice*.

You'll see that, as with bullets and numbering, there's a toolbar below the document for Tables. Click ⊞. The unwanted blank row is deleted.

Click on *Libreoffice* or use the arrow keys to move to it. Change the *o* to *O*.

Oops again! We forgot about WordPad. Click on *Gedit* or use the arrow keys to move to it. Click ⊞ in the Table toolbar. A blank row is inserted between *Notepad* and *LibreOffice*. Type *WordPad, Yes, No* and *No* into it.

> *Gedit is a text editor included with Ubuntu. WordPad is a simple word processor that's included with Microsoft Windows.*

> *The Table toolbar has many other buttons with tool-tips including ones for inserting and deleting columns and changing the style of the lines. You can experiment.*

If you place the cursor over the line between columns in the table, it changes to a line and two arrows. You can drag it from side to side to change the width of the columns.

Click just before the first *No* in the *Gedit* row. Drag down to after the last *Yes* in the *Microsoft Word* row. All the *No*'s and *Yes*'s are highlighted. Click 🔲. They are centred under their headings.

You can select single or multiple entries in a table and change their justification, typeface, size and style just like any other text.

Click below the table. The Table toolbar disappears. Click 🅰 or press the CTRL+B shortcut and type *Word Processor features*. Click 🔲 to centre the caption.

If you fit either description, this book is meant for you.

Program	Formatting	Styles	Grammar
Gedit	No	No	No
WordPad	Yes	No	No
LibreOffice	Yes	Yes	No
Microsoft Word	Yes	Yes	Yes

Word Processor features

What you learned:

- **How to insert a blank table.**
- **That there's a toolbar for tables.**
- **How to type text into the table.**
- **How to delete and insert rows in the table.**
- **How to edit text in the table.**
- **How to format text in the table.**
- *What happens if the table won't fit on the current page.*
- *How to change the style of the lines in the table.*
- *How to adjust the width of the table columns.*

7.8 Adding a table of contents

Place the text cursor before the title of Chapter 1 (*Introduction*). Click on *Insert > Indexes and Tables > Indexes and Tables....*

The *Insert Index/Table* dialogue box appears, already set up for a Table of Contents. Note the *Evaluate up to level* box on the *Index/Table* tab. Your document has levels *1* (chapters) and *2* (sections) – these were set up in the *Tools > Outline Numbering...* dialogue. So long as the box is set to *2* or higher, the table of contents will show both chapters and sections in each chapter. If you wanted to only show the chapters, you could set the box to *1*.

Click [OK]. The table is created. It shows the chapters and chapter sections in your document, complete with page numbers:

Table of Contents

You can mark words or phrases as entries for an alphabetic index by selecting one of them and clicking Insert > Indexes and Tables > Entry.... A dialogue box opens with the selected word(s) as the Entry. You can specify other words as 1st and 2nd keys, e.g. with the Entry as left button, set the 1st key as mouse. Click [Insert] to mark the word: it becomes shown with a highlighted background.

The dialogue box stays open. You can select another word in the document, perhaps keeping the same 1st and 2nd keys. The Entry doesn't have to match the text in the document. For example, you might select right and change the Entry to right button. Click [Insert] again.

Once you've marked the index entries, click [Close] to close the dialogue box. Click where you want the index to go in the document, then click Insert > Indexes and Tables > Indexes and Tables.... A dialogue box opens. Select Alphabetical Index as the Type on the Index/Table tab. Click [OK]. The index is created. With the example entries above, the index would include mouse with sub-entries for left button and right button.

You can set up a cross-reference (e.g. See Page 1234) by clicking where you want the reference to point to. Click Insert > Cross-reference.... A dialogue box opens. Make sure Set Reference is highlighted in the Type section and type a name

that you'll recognise later in the Name box. Click `Insert` *,
then* `Close` *.*

*Click where you want the cross-reference to appear, then click
Insert > Cross-reference.... In the dialogue box Type section,
click to highlight Insert Reference. In Selection, click on the
name you chose earlier. In Insert reference to, choose if you
want to show the page or chapter number or the word above or
below. Click* `Insert` *.*

What you learned:

- **How to create a table of contents.**

- **How quick and easy this is if you use paragraph styles and
outline numbering.**

- *How to create an index and cross-references that are easily
updated when you make changes.*

7.9 Giving the document a title

Click *File > Properties....* A dialogue box opens. Click on the *Description* tab and type *Mini book* into the *Title* box.

*You can set other information on various tabs. This information,
which doesn't appear in the document itself unless you insert it
as a field, is known as* **meta-data**.

Click on the *Statistics* tab. You see information about the document
including a word count.

*You can see the word count more easily by clicking Tools >
Word Count.*

Click `OK`.

What you learned:

- **How to set document meta-data, including a title.**

- **How to see statistics about the document, including a word
count.**

- *What meta-data is.*

7.10 Adding a footer or header and fields

Click *Insert > Footer > Default*. A footer is added at the bottom of the page. Click at the very bottom of any page to place the text cursor in the footer.

Click *Insert > Fields > Other....* A dialogue window appears. Click on the *Document* tab. Click on *Chapter* in the *Type* box and *Chapter number and name* in the *Format* box. Click Insert , then Close .

Press TAB, then type *Page* and press SPACEBAR. Click *Insert > Fields > Page Number*. Press SPACEBAR, type *of* and press SPACEBAR again. Click *Insert > Fields > Page Count*.

> *You'll see that a Centred tab stop (* ⊥ *) was created automatically on the ruler so that the page numbers are centred in the footer. You can drag* ⊥ *off the ruler. This puts the title at the left side and the page numbers at the right.*

Look through the document. You'll see that there's a footer on each page showing the appropriate chapter number and name and the page number.

> *When you insert a field, it brings in information from somewhere else such as the current chapter name or page number or information from the document properties. You can insert fields anywhere in your document, not just in a footer or header.*
>
> *Fields are shown on the screen with a grey background but this doesn't appear when the document is printed.*

The table of contents and footers don't update automatically if you add pages or change a chapter title. Click *Tools > Update > Update All*.

> *This updates indexes and cross-references too, including adding newly marked entries to an index you'd already inserted.*
>
> *You can create a header at the top of each page instead of or as well as a footer. In the Insert menu, position the mouse cursor over Header. A box appears. Click on Default.*
>
> *To delete a header or footer, position the mouse cursor over Header or Footer in the Insert menu. You'll see a tick next to Default showing that there's currently a header or footer. Click on it. You'll see a warning that anything in the header or footer will be deleted. Click* Yes .

If you want to change a footer to a header or vice-versa, you can create the new header or footer, select the text in the old one and use cut and paste (CTRL+X and CTRL+V) to move it to the new one before you delete the old one.

What you learned:

- **How to add headers and footers to every page.**
- **How to use fields to insert information that's calculated or updated automatically.**
- **How to update information everywhere, including the Table of Contents.**
- *That you can insert fields anywhere in the document.*
- *That fields appear with a normal background when the document is printed.*

7.11 Exporting a PDF file

If you want to send your document to someone else, you can send it as a **PDF (Portable Document Format)** file. This has advantages:

- The recipient doesn't need to have LibreOffice or any other word processor.
- Most computers and even many smartphones already have a PDF viewing program installed and, if not, it's free to download and install.
- The document will appear and print out exactly as you intended, even if the recipient doesn't have the same fonts installed.
- The recipient normally won't be able to edit the document: this could be an advantage or a disadvantage.

To export a PDF file, click ▣ (next to 🖨). A dialogue box appears where you can choose the location and name of the file. Click ▢ Save ▢ . The document is exported.

Whether you want to send the document as a PDF file or as a LibreOffice Writer or Microsoft Word file, you can copy the file to a disk or thumbdrive and give it to the recipient or you can attach it to an e-mail and send it to them.

What you learned:

- **What a PDF file is and what's needed to open it.**
- **That even many smartphones can be used to view PDF files.**
- **That a document sent as a PDF file will appear exactly as you intended but it cannot be edited.**
- **How to export a document as a PDF file.**

7.12 Saving as a different file type

Microsoft Word 2010 can open Writer (.odt) files but older versions can't. You'll want to save a document as a Word file if you're going to send it to a Word user.

Click *File > Save As....* The *Save As* dialogue box appears. Type *Mini book* into the *Name:* box and click *Documents* at the left side. Double click on the *WP files* folder to choose it as the destination. and click ⎡ Save ⎤. The document is saved in *WP files* in the LibreOffice Writer format.

As you saw in Section 5.14, until you give the document a name clicking 🖫 also opens the Save As dialogue box.

Click *File > Save As....* The *Save As* dialogue box appears again. Click ⎡↕⎤ above ⎡ Save ⎤ and click on *Microsoft Word 97/2000/XP/2003 (.doc)* in the list.

You can move the cursor over the triangle below the list to scroll down.

Now only files of that type appear in the list of files (there may not be any). Check that you're in the *WP files* folder and that *Mini book* is shown in the *Name:* box, then click ⎡ Save ⎤.

You may see a warning message that some formatting or content cannot be saved in the Microsoft Word file format. Click ⎡ Use Microsoft Word 97/2000/XP/2003 Format ⎤.

Click ⓧ to close Writer.

If you have access to Microsoft Word and try opening the file with it, you may see a few glitches: e.g. the headers and footers may be wrong. Similar problems can happen when a Writer .odt file is opened in Word 2010.

Writer can open as well as save Microsoft Word files but even it may have minor problems when it opens the Word version of Mini book. That's why it warned you when you saved the document in Word format. (You could safely ignore the warning this time because you'd already saved it in LibreOffice format too.)

Writer can save documents as many other file types. **Rich Text Format (.rtf)** *files can be opened with almost any word processor but anything more than the simplest text formatting may be lost.* **Text (.txt)** *is the simplest file type of all – it's just an electronic version of the paper tape in Chapter 2. The words in your document are saved but all formatting is lost.*

Writer can open even more file formats than it can save. Old **WordPerfect** *or* **Quattro Pro** *files? No problem.*

What you learned:

- **How to save your document in Microsoft Word format.**
- *That Microsoft Word itself can cope with most of the formatting in in your document.*
- *That LibreOffice Writer can open Microsoft Word files.*
- *That LibreOffice Writer can save and open documents of many other file types.*

7.13 Templates

If you often make similar documents, for example if you need to write a monthly report, wouldn't it be nice to be able to start a new version with the paragraph styles and header or footer already set up? Not only would this save time, it would also help to keep new versions consistent in style with the previous ones.

When starting a new version, you could open a previous version, delete all the text that's not going to be needed in the new version, click *File > Save As...* to set the file name for the new version, then start typing the new text. This means having to delete a lot of stuff every time you start a new version of the document and there's the risk that you'll forget to rename it and lose the old version when you save the new one.

The better way is, after saving the document, to delete everything that won't be needed in future versions, then save it again as a **template** file. Click *File > Save As...* and choose *ODF Text Document Template (.ott)* as the file type.

Ubuntu knows this is a different type of file with a different extension (*.ott* instead of *.odt*). The existing document file won't be overwritten even if the template file has the same name.

> *The file **extension** is the part, usually three or four letters, following the dot at the end of its name. Windows computers rely on the extension to know what type of file it is: they may also hide the extension itself when they show the file name.*

When you want to make a new document based on it, open the template file in exactly the same way as you would open the document file. Ubuntu knows to use LibreOffice Writer to open this type of file. Writer knows that, when you open a template file, you're starting a new document. When you click 🖫 or *File > Save*, you'll be asked to give your document file a new name.

What you learned:

- **When a template file is useful.**
- **How to prepare and save a template file.**
- **That, when you open a template file, Writer knows you are starting a new document and will make sure you give it a name when you save it.**
- *What a file extension is.*

8 Spreadsheets

Did you ever try to add up a column of numbers but got a different answer every time?

A spreadsheet is a powerful tool when you need to work with numbers. Not only does it do complicated calculations in a flash, it does them consistently and it records exactly how you set up the calculations for future reference.

This chapter is an introduction to the LibreOffice Calc spreadsheet.

Other spreadsheet programs such as Microsoft Excel are very similar.

8.1 Starting LibreOffice Calc

Click ▦ on the Launcher. The LibreOffice Calc spreadsheet program starts and a window appears on the screen.

The **spreadsheet** looks a bit like a table with columns and rows of **cells**. You'll notice the column headers: these identify each column with a different letter (*A, B, C...*). The rows are identified with numbers (*1, 2, 3...*). A cell can be specified by giving its column letter and row number. E.g. the top left cell is *A1*. Cell *B1* is to its right and cell *A2* is below it.

Click on cell *A1*. Its border is emphasised. Type *Ingredient* and press TAB. Cell *B1* is emphasised. Type *Amount* and press TAB. Cell *C1* is emphasised. Type *Price each* and press TAB. Cell *D1* is emphasised. Type *Cost*.

You might want to look at the screenshot below.

Click on cell *A2* (below *A1*) so its border is highlighted. Type *Flour (kg)* and press RETURN. Cell *A3* is emphasised. Type *Sugar (kg)* and press RETURN. Cell *A4* is highlighted. Type *Eggs*.

TAB moves to the next cell to the right. RETURN moves to the cell below. SHIFT+TAB moves to the cell to the left and SHIFT+RETURN moves to the cell above.

Type *0.5* in cell *B2*, *0.3* in cell *B3* and *2* in cell B4. Type *1.1* in cell *C2*,

1.8 in cell *C3* and *0.25* in cell *C4*.

Type *=B2*C2* in cell *D2* and press RETURN. *D2* shows *0.55*.

> *A cell can contain text (words), a number or a* **formula***. A formula starts with = and it can* **refer** *to other cells in the spreadsheet. In this case, the formula says to multiply together the numbers in cells B2 and C2 (amount and price), giving 0.55.*

> *A formula can contain numbers. In a formula, * multiplies, / divides and ^ raises to a power. For example, =6*2 would show 12, =6/2 would show 3 and =6^2 would show 36 (6 squared).*

Click on cell *D2* and press CTRL+C. The formula is copied to the clipboard.

Drag the mouse cursor over cells *D3* and *D4*. Both cells are highlighted. Press CTRL+V. The formula is pasted into these cells.

Click in cell *D3*. You can see the formula it contains in the box at the top of the spreadsheet (circled below). It's *=B3*C3* rather than *=B2*C2* and the value of cell *D3* (*0.54*) is different from that of cell *D2*.

> *When you paste a formula into a cell, any cells that it refers to are usually adjusted according to where the cell is relative to the original one. In Section 8.3 you'll see how to set an absolute reference where this doesn't happen.*

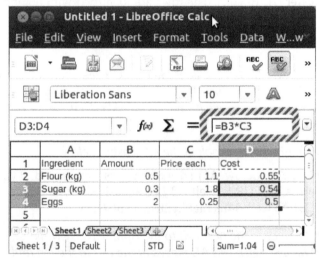

Don't try making this cake. It'd probably be revolting!

What you learned:

- **What a spreadsheet cell is and how it's identified and referenced.**

- **That a cell can contain text, a number or a formula.**

- **That the value calculated by a formula is automatically shown in the cell.**

- **That the formula itself is shown in the box above the spreadsheet.**

- **That a formula can use the values of other cells (references).**

- **That a formula can be copied and pasted into additional cells.**

- **That, when this is done, any cell references in the formula are adjusted so they are relative to the new cell location.**

- *That you can use numbers as well as cell references in a formula.*

- *How to use TAB, RETURN and SHIFT to move to an adjacent cell.*

8.2 Using functions and inserting rows and columns

Click in cell *B6* and type *SUBTOTAL*. Click in cell *D6* and type *=sum(*. Don't press TAB or RETURN.

Drag the mouse cursor over cells *D2* to *D4*. They are highlighted. Type *)*. You see that the formula in cell *D6* is *=sum(D2:D4)*. Press RETURN. The value in cell *D6* is now *1.59*.

This formula uses Calc's built-in *SUM* function to add the values of cells *D2*, *D4* and any cells in between them. Dragging over these cells automatically puts the **cell range** into the formula. You could have typed it in as *D2:D4* instead.

> *Calc provides many other functions. For example, you can find the minimum, maximum or average value of a range of cells. Mathematical and trigonometric functions are available.*
>
> *Insert > Function List opens a pane at the right hand side showing you available functions. Click Insert > Function List again to get rid of the pane.*

Click *Help > LibreOffice Help*. The **Help** window opens. Click on the *Index* tab and type *sum* into the *Search term* box. Double-click on *SUM* *function* in the list of topics below. Information about the function is shown.

> *LibreOffice has a comprehensive though not always comprehensible help system. Try it for any other questions you have.*

The Help window is separate from your document. You can resize, move and minimise it. Click on its ⊗ to close it. Your document remains open.

> *Clicking Help > About LibreOffice opens a window with information including the exact version of LibreOffice that's installed. This is useful if you want to know if you have the newest version or need technical support. Most programs have similar Help menus.*

Click cell *B1*. Hold down SHIFT and click cell *D1*. The two cells along with *C1* are highlighted.

> *You can select multiple cells in the spreadsheet just like you select text (Section 5.6) or files in a folder (Section 6.6).*

> *Holding down CTRL lets you add a cell to an existing selection.*

> *Holding down SHIFT and clicking extends the selection by adding the new cell along with any cells in between.*

Click ⊒. The contents of the selected cells become right justified.

Click on the number *1* to the left of the top row of cells. The whole row is highlighted.

Click ⒜. The contents of the highlighted cells are now in bold.

> *You can use the buttons and drop-down lists to change the typeface, size and style of cell contents, just as in LibreOffice Writer.*

Click *Insert > Rows*. A new row of cells is added above the highlighted one.

Click ⒜ so it's no longer highlighted.

Click cell *B2*. Hold down SHIFT and click cell *D7*. All the cells in rows *2-7* of columns *B*, *C* and *D* (a **rectangular area**) are highlighted. Drag them one column to the right.

You can insert rows or columns or drag a block of cells to make room for new entries.

References are automatically changed when rows or columns are inserted or cells are dragged. For example, the formula in cell E3 is =C3*D3. It was originally entered as =B2*C2 in cell D2.

What you learned:

- **How to use a built-in function in a formula.**
- **How to use the LibreOffice Help menu.**
- **How to specify a range of cells or select them by dragging.**
- **How to select an entire row or column of cells.**
- **How to change the font (typeface, style and size) used to display cell contents.**
- **How to insert a row of blank cells.**
- **How to select cells in a rectangular area.**
- **How to move selected cells by dragging.**
- *That Calc has many built-in functions that you can see using Insert > Function List.*
- *That references are automatically changed when you insert rows or columns or drag and drop cells.*
- *How to find the versions of LibreOffice and other programs on your computer.*

8.3 Column widths and absolute references

Click cell *A1* and type *Cakes per batch*. Click cell *C1* and type *10*.

Click cell *B2*, click ▲, type *Amount per cake* and press TAB.

Cell C2 is now highlighted. We want to change its contents from *Amount* to *Amount per batch*. Click after *Amount* in the box above the spreadsheet that shows the cell contents and press SPACEBAR. Type *per batch* and press RETURN. Cell C2 is updated.

Cakes per batch in cell *A1* is shown correctly even though it spills into cell *A2*. However *Amount per cake* and *Amount per batch* are truncated because the adjacent cells aren't blank. Place the mouse cursor between B and C above these columns. The cursor changes to a double-headed arrow. Drag to the right. Column *B* becomes wider. Widen it enough so that *Amount per cake* is shown properly.

Repeat this procedure to widen column *C* so that *Amount per batch* is shown correctly.

Click cell *C3* and drag down to cell *C5*. Cells *C3*, *C4* and *C5* are highlighted. Press CTRL+C. Click on cell B3 and press CTRL+V. The contents of cells *C3-C5* are copied to cells *B3-B5*.

> *Moving instead of copying these cells would change the references to them in column E. We don't want that to happen.*

Click cell *C3*, type *=c$1*b3* and press RETURN. Click cell *C3* again. Note that the letters *b* and *c* in the formula are automatically changed to *B* and *C* – you don't need to press SHIFT when typing references or function names in a formula.

Press CTRL+C. Highlight cells *C4* and *C5* and press CTRL+V. You're asked if you really want to overwrite existing data in the cells. Click <kbd>Yes</kbd>.

> *Note that the values shown in cells C3-C5 are all 10 times larger than the numbers in cells B3-B5.*

If you click on cells C3, C4 and C5 in turn, you'll see that the formulas are *=C$1*B3*, *=C$1*B4* and *=C$1*B5* respectively. The *$* in *C$1* made it an **absolute reference** telling the spreadsheet to always refer to the cell in row *1*, even when the formula is pasted into other cells lower (or higher) in the same column.

> *If you wanted to paste the formula into cells in different columns, you could put $ in front of the letter in the reference. E.g. the formula =C1*B3 would always refer to cell C1 no matter where it was pasted into the spreadsheet.*

What you learned:

- **How to modify the contents of a cell.**
- **How to change the width of a column.**
- **How to specify an absolute reference to another cell that doesn't change when the formula is copied and pasted.**
- **That you don't have to press SHIFT when you type a cell reference.**

8.4 Calculations, currencies and merged cells

Click cell *B9*. Type *Mark-up* and press TAB. Click **%** on the Calc toolbar, type *76*, click ⚏ (also on the toolbar) twice and press TAB twice. Type *=e7*c9* and press RETURN.

> *You've formatted cell C9 as a* **percentage** *and set it to 76. Calc show this as 76% and the actual value of the cell becomes 0.76 (76/100).*

Click cell *B10* and type *Batch Price*. Click cell *E10* and type = (don't press TAB or RETURN). Click cell *E7*, type + and click cell *E9*. The formula shows as *=E7+E9*. Press RETURN.

> *When you're entering or editing cell contents, you can insert a reference to another cell by clicking on it.*

Click on cell *B11* and type *Postage*. Click on cell *E11* and type *5*.

Click on cell *B12* and type *Price per cake*. Click on cell *E12* and type *=e11+e10/c1*. Press RETURN.

Cell E12 shows *7.7984* but that's plainly wrong. The batch price plus postage is just over £30 so the cost per cake should be about £3, not almost £8.

> *It's always a good idea to look at the result of a calculation to see if it looks plausible.*

This error happened because Calc calculates values from formulas using algebraic conventions. Multiplications and divisions are done before additions and subtractions. Calc is dividing the batch price (*E10*) by the number of cakes, then adding the whole postage charge (*E11*). You need to add brackets (parentheses) so that Calc does the addition before the division.

Click on cell *E12*. Click after = in the formula in the box above the spreadsheet and type *(.* Press the right arrow key repeatedly until the cursor is just before / in the formula. Type *).* The formula reads *=(E11+E10)/C1*. Press RETURN. The price is now 3.2984.

> *When you're editing cell content, the left and right arrow keys move the cursor backwards and forwards. At other times, they change your position in the spreadsheet.*

The costs and prices are a bit of a mess. Surely they should be in pounds and whole pence (or dollars or Euros and whole cents)?

Click on the letter *D* above the third column of cells. The whole column is highlighted. Hold down CTRL and click on the letter *E* at the top of the fourth column. Both columns are now highlighted.

Click *Format > Cells....* A dialogue box appears. Click on the *Numbers* tab. Click on *Currency* in the *Category* box, then click [OK]. All numbers in columns *C* and *D* are now formatted as **currency** amounts. The way they appear depends on your location settings: they will usually show the symbol for your local currency and the appropriate number of digits of minor units (e.g. 2 digits for pence or cents).

> *You can select various currencies on the Numbers tab.*

> *The price per cake is now shown as £3.30 instead of 3.2984. Calc rounds the amount to the nearest penny.*

Click on the number *1* to the left of the top row of cells and click *Insert > Rows*. A new row of cells is added above the highlighted row.

Select the new cells *A1* to *E1*. Click *Format > Merge cells > Merge and Center cells*. Cells *A1* to *M1* are merged into one. Click in the merged cell, type *CAKE PRICE CALCULATION* and press RETURN.

Select cells *B4* to *B6* (e.g. by dragging). Hold down CTRL and select cells D4 to D6. While still holding down CTRL, click on cells *C2*, *C10* and *E12*. You've selected all the cells with numbers (rather than text or formulas) in them. Release CTRL and click 🅰.

> *Numbers that you might want to twiddle later are now in **bold**.*

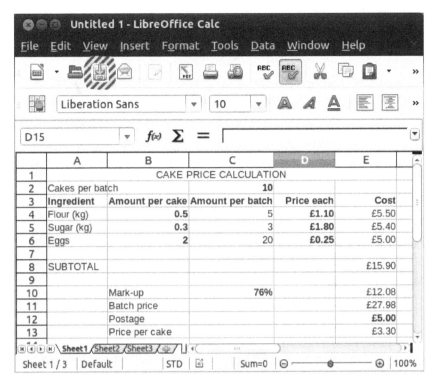

What you learned:

- What happens when you format a cell as a percentage.
- A quick way to change the number of digits shown after the decimal point.
- That you can enter a cell reference in a formula by clicking on the cell.
- That the order of calculations follows algebraic conventions.
- That you can use brackets (parentheses) to change the order of calculations in a formula.
- That you can use the left and right arrow keys when you're editing a formula.
- That you can add cells to an existing selection by holding down CTRL.
- How to format cells so they show their values as currency amounts.
- How to merge cells when you need more space.

- *That you can use the four arrow keys to move around the spreadsheet.*
- *How to format cells to show different currencies.*
- *That values are automatically rounded (e.g. to pence) when shown as a currency.*

8.5 Saving the spreadsheet

Click 🖫 (circled above). A dialogue box appears which is similar to the one you see when saving a LibreOffice Writer document.

As with Writer, type the file name, e.g. *Cakes*. Click [Save].

> *Spreadsheets can be saved in various formats including Microsoft Excel 97/2000/XP/2003 (.xls).*

What you learned:

- **How to save a spreadsheet file.**
- *That the spreadsheet can be saved in Microsoft Excel format.*

8.6 Using the spreadsheet

You can change any of the numbers (formatted in bold) and the spreadsheet updates immediately. You can change the number of cakes per batch, the amount or cost of each ingredient, the mark-up percentage or the postage and see the effect.

> *If you change numbers in the spreadsheet just to see what happens, you'll be warned that the changes haven't been saved when you close Calc. Provided that you saved the spreadsheet before you started twiddling the figures and you don't want to save the latest figures you entered, you can click [Discard].*

What you learned:

- **That the whole spreadsheet is updated immediately when you change any value in it.**

9 Charts and Sorting

This chapter covers some more advanced spreadsheet functions including handling dates, sorting rows and making charts (graphs).

The spreadsheet you make in this chapter will also be used in Chapters 10 and 13.

Start LibreOffice Calc. A new spreadsheet opens. Fill in cells *A1* to *C11* with data as follows:

	A	B	C
1	**Title**	**First name**	**Surname**
2	mr	riley	holt
3	mr	zachary	vincent
4	mrs	chloe	vincent
5	ms	elise	gill
6	mr	kieran	kirby
7	mr	taylor	bevan
8	mrs	tilly	north
9	mr	ellis	holt
10	miss	faith	bibi
11	mr	andrew	holland

Don't bother typing capitals in rows 2 to 11.

Fill in cells *D1* to *F11* as follows:

	D	E	F
1	**Address**	**Town**	**Postcode**
2	52 asfordby rd	aldbrough	dl11 5dl
3	58 netherpark cr	stetchworth	cb8 0hz
4	79 essex rd	tarbert	hs3 4rc
5	92 gloddaeth st	bircham tofts	pe31 0or
6	89 sandyhill rd	gaer	np8 3fj
7	59 western tce	miserden	gl6 4or
8	46 hindhead rd	eardington	wv16 1co
9	22 circle way	caerau	cf34 5yn
10	25 trinity cr	wheedlemont	ab54 8hc
11	63 ivy lane	wardgate	de6 5ii

Fill in cells *G1* to *I11* as follows:

	G	H	I
1	**Born**	**Height**	**Weight**
2	2/11/40	188	112.1
3	2/4/28	170	88.9
4	9/4/78	156	50.6
5	8/4/81	166	62.4
6	11/8/49	179	109.5
7	9/3/69	170	66.7
8	7/3/43	174	98.4
9	12/5/46	173	84
10	1/6/42	170	59
11	4/12/72	187	87.3

The whole table wouldn't fit in the book: that's why it's in three chunks.

Dates are deliberately chosen so that they appear valid in either American (m/d/y) or European (d/m/y) format. Heights are in centimetres and weights in kilograms.

Select cells *A2* to *D11* so that they are highlighted. Click *Format > Change case > Capitalise Every Word*. Select cells *E2* to *F11* and click *Format > Change case > UPPERCASE*. Everything is now nicely capitalised. (LibreOffice Writer has the same options to change the capitalisation of highlighted text.)

Select cells *A1* to *I11* so that they are highlighted. Click *Format > Column > Optimal Width....* A dialogue box opens. Click OK . The column widths are adjusted automatically to suit the selected cells.

Click 🖫 and save the spreadsheet as *People*.

You don't want to have to type all that stuff in again if something goes wrong.

What you learned:

- **That a spreadsheet can be used to make a simple table of data (e.g. names and addresses).**
- **How tedious it can be to type in names and addresses.**
- **How to get Calc to automatically adjust column widths.**
- **How to change the capitalisation of text in Calc and Writer.**

9.1 Making an x-y (scatter) chart

Are the heights and weights of people in this table related?

Drag to select cells *I4* and *I5*. Release, then drag the cells to *J4* and *J5*. Select cells *I8* and *J8*. Release, then drag them to *J8* and *K8*. Repeat to move cells *I10* and *J10* to *J10* and *K10*.

> *You can move cells by dragging but only when two or more adjacent cells are selected. E.g. you had to select blank cell J8 before you could drag I8.*

Now the men have their weights in column *I* and the women's weights are in column *J*. Change cell *I1* to *Men* and cell *J1* to *Women*.

Drag to select cells *H1* to *J11*. Click *Insert > Chart....* The **Chart Wizard** appears. It's a rather intimidating looking dialogue box.

> *A **Wizard** guides you through some complicated procedure.*

Click on Chart type *XY (Scatter)* to select it. You can click ⬚ Finish ⬚ right away. The chart is created.

Position the mouse cursor over the rectangular grey outline of the chart and drag it down and to the left until its top left covers cell A13. Right-click inside the grey outline and choose *Insert Titles....*

A dialogue box opens. Type *Height (cm)* into the first *X axis* box and *Weight (kg)* into the first *Y axis* box. Click ⬚ OK ⬚ .

The X-Y chart is now nicely set up. There's a dot for each person. Its horizontal position shows their height and its vertical position shows their weight. It shows that the men are generally taller than the women and that the taller people tend to be heavier.

> *Scandal! These people don't really exist. The data you're using is completely fake and has been chosen to make the chart look plausible.*

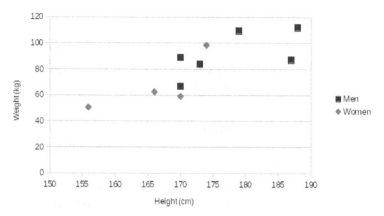

It would be interesting to see these people's *Body Mass Index*.

Click cell *K1* and type *BMI*. Click cell *K2* and type *=10000*i2/h2^2*.

> *Body Mass Index is the person's weight in kilograms divided by the square of their height in metres. The ^2 tells Calc to square the value of H2. You need to multiply by 10,000 (100²) because the heights are recorded in centimetres rather than metres.*

Copy and paste the formula in cell *K2* into cells *K3-11*.

There's a problem: the women's weights are in a different column and their BMIs are shown as zero. Click on an incorrect cell, then on the formula in the box at the top. Cells in column *H* and *I* are highlighted in different colours, indicating that they are used in the formula. Put the mouse cursor over the highlighted cell in column *I* and drag it across to column *J*. Press RETURN. The BMI is now correct.

Repeat to fix the BMIs for the other three women.

The BMI values are ridiculously precise. Select cells *K2* to *K11* and click *Format > Cells*. A dialogue box appears. Click on the *Numbers* tab, then, in the *Format* box, click on *-1234.12*. Change *Decimal places* from *2* to *1*. Click　OK　. The BMI values are rounded to one digit after the decimal point, e.g. 30.8 for Mr. Vincent instead of 30.761246.

> *Instead of using Format > Cells, you could just click 🔢 a number of times.*

> *Rounding set either way only affects the values when they are shown. It doesn't affect the results of formulas elsewhere that refer to those cells. E.g. if you enter =K3 as a formula in cell L3, you'll still see 30.761246 there. If you wanted to round the value*

in references to 1 decimal place too, you could use
=round(10000*i2/h2^2, 1) as the formula in K2.

What you learned:

- **What an X-Y (scatter) chart is and how to create one.**

- **How to add captions to the chart axes.**

- **How to move the chart to where you want it.**

- **That cell references in a formula can be changed by dragging.**

- **Two ways to format cells to show a different number of digits after the decimal point.**

- *That this doesn't affect the value of the cell, only the way it's shown.*

- *That you can use the built-in ROUND() function to round a value in or result of a formula.*

- *What a Wizard is.*

9.2 Date and time calculations

The normal range for BMI is 18.5 to 25. Some of the people are overweight. We'll calculate their ages and see if "middle age spread" is the problem.

Click on cell *K1*. Click *Insert > Columns*. A new column is inserted. Type *Age* into the new blank cell *K1*. Type *=now()-g2* into cell *K2* and press RETURN.

You see a meaningless date in *K2*. With *K2* selected, click *Format > Cells....* On the *Number* tab, set *Category* to *number*, *Format* to *-1234* and click OK . The cell now shows a huge number which is still pretty meaningless.

Change the formula in cell K2 to *=int((NOW()-G2)/365.25)* and press RETURN. The cell shows Mr. Holt's age correctly.

The NOW() function gives the current date and time when the cell is edited or a saved spreadsheet is opened. The date and time is in days since the start of 30 December 1899: the fractional part gives the time of day. For example, midday on 1 January 1900 is represented by the number 2.5.

If a cell contains something that looks like a date and/or time, Calc automatically converts it to a number and formats the cell so that it interprets the number in a format similar to what you entered (it may not be exactly the same). When you enter a time without a date, it's converted to a number between 0 and 1, as if it was that time on 30 December 1899. When you enter a date without a time, it's converted to a whole number as if the day had just started.

You can tell Calc to display any number as if it's a date and/or time of day. There's a wide choice of formats on the Numbering tab.

You can add or subtract cells containing dates and times, e.g. to see how much time has elapsed between two dates and times or when some number of days will have elapsed. No need to account for how many days there are in each month.

We want the ages in years rather than days so we need to divide by the number of days in a year. We're using 365.25 days to account for leap years.

We also want to see the person's age at their last birthday. If someone is 29 years and 8 months old, we want to see 29, not 29.67 or 30 (which is 29.67 rounded to the nearest whole number). The INT() function rounds numbers down.

The result will still be wrong very occasionally because of our simplification of leap years.

You might input something that Calc thinks is a date or time, and tries to convert when it shouldn't. For example, suppose you note the terms of a loan by typing APR 10 into a cell. Calc interprets this as a date. You can prevent this or other attempts to interpret a text string as a number or formula by starting it with a single quote, e.g. 'APR 10.

Copy the formula in cell *K2* into cells *K3-K11* so that everyone's age is shown.

Oops! Mr. Vincent's age is negative!

When you enter a date with a two digit year (e.g. 2/4/28), Calc guesses the century. It uses a cut-off year. For example, if the cut-off year is 1930, it assumes years 30-99 are in the 20th

*century (1930-1999) and years 00-29 are in the 21st century
(2000-2029). It thinks Mr. Vincent isn't born yet.*

*The cut-off date can be changed by clicking Tools > Options,
then clicking ▶ next to LibreOffice in the dialogue box that
appears and clicking on General. There are many other options
that can be set in the dialogue box.*

Click cell *G3* and enter the date of birth as *2/4/1928*. His age is now
correct.

What you learned:

- **How Calc records, calculates and shows dates and times.**
- **That Calc can't always correctly interpret years entered as
  two digits.**
- *How to determine the current date and time.*
- *How to round down a calculation result.*
- *How to display dates and times in the way you want.*
- *How to calculate elapsed times or when a time will have
  elapsed.*
- *How to tell Calc that a string is text and to not try to interpret
  it.*
- *How to change the cut-off year and set various other
  LibreOffice options.*

9.3 Making a column chart

Select cells *K1* to *L11*. Click *Insert > Chart*. The Chart Wizard appears
again. Chart type *Column* should already be selected: if not, click on it.
Click   Finish . The chart is created. Position the mouse cursor
over the rectangular grey outline of the new chart and drag it down so
it's to the right of the X-Y chart.

*The chart shows the ten people in order with two bars for each
person. One indicates their age and the other indicates their
BMI. There might be a relationship but it isn't at all clear.*

Select cells *A2* to *L11*. Click *Data > Sort....* A dialogue box appears.
Set the top *Sort by* box to *Column K*. Leave the other two boxes set to
-undefined-. Click   OK .

Be sure to select all the columns required before sorting data. If you miss some out, they'll be left unchanged and will become associated with the wrong records.

The selected rows are sorted by increasing age and the chart updates.

When you choose a column for sorting, it can contain numeric values or text. Text is sorted alphabetically. For example, you could choose Column C to sort the people by surname but there are two people with the surname Holt and two with Vincent. You could choose column B as the second sort column so that people with the same surname are sorted by their first name. For each column you choose, you can reverse the sort order (e.g. 10 to 1 or Z to A) by clicking the Descending radio button.

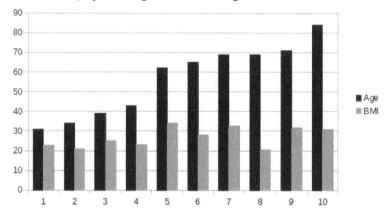

The chart shows some slight evidence of middle age spread. A lot more people would have to be added before we could say for sure.

Click to update the saved spreadsheet. You'll be using it again.

We've only briefly touched on the different types of chart and the ways to smarten them up. There are a great many options that can be set in the Chart Wizard and charts can be modified after they have been created. You may want to experiment.

What you learned:

- **What a column chart is and how to make one.**
- **How to quickly sort data stored in a Calc spreadsheet.**
- *That you can select a text column to sort data alphabetically.*
- *To be careful when selecting the columns to be sorted.*

- *That there's a lot more you can learn about charts.*

10 Graphics and pages

In this chapter, you'll use Writer to write a report based on what you found out in Chapter 9. The report will include the charts from the spreadsheet and will show the raw data as an embedded spreadsheet that looks like a table when it's printed.

This chapter may be most useful to students.

10.1 Pasting graphics and data from the spreadsheet

Start LibreOffice Writer. A new blank document opens.

Leaving the Writer document open and unsaved, open *People.ods* (the spreadsheet you made in Chapter 9). You may be able to do this by going to *File > Recent Documents...* in Writer and clicking on *People.ods*. Otherwise, click ▨ on the Launcher, go to *Documents* and open it.

> *Both the new Writer document and the People spreadsheet are now in your computer's RAM and the LibreOffice Writer and Calc programs are multitasking (Section 4.2). You can switch between them by clicking their icons on the Launcher or by clicking the LibreOffice Window menu and clicking on the one you want.*
>
> *You can also switch programs and documents by holding down the ALT key and pressing TAB. The first time you press TAB, you'll see all your running programs in a box in the middle of the screen. One of them will be highlighted. Each time you press TAB again, the highlight moves to the next program. When it's on the one you want, release ALT.*

Click on the X-Y chart of weight versus height that you made in Section 9.1. Use CTRL+C to copy it to the clipboard.

Click ▨ on the Launcher or use the *Window* menu or ALT+TAB to switch to your new untitled Writer document. It reappears. Press CTRL+V. The X-Y chart is pasted into the document.

Switch back to the *People* spreadsheet, click on the column chart of ages and BMIs that you made in Section 9.3 and copy it to the clipboard.

Switch to the new Writer document, click so that the text cursor is flashing below the X-Y chart and press CTRL+V. The column chart is pasted into the document.

Switch to the *People* spreadsheet. Select cells *B1* to *L11* (a rectangular area) and press CTRL+C to copy it to the clipboard.

Switch to the new Writer document, click so that the text cursor is flashing below the column chart and press CTRL+V. The selected cells are pasted into the document.

Make sure you can see all of the pasted cells with some space around them. You may need to click ⊝ a few times and use the scrollbars.

Double-click on the cells. They open as a spreadsheet **object embedded** in your Writer document. It has its own scrollbars (arrowed below) and you can edit it as if you were using Calc.

	B	C	D	E	F	G	H	I	J	K	L
	First name	Surname	Address	Town	Postcode	Born	Height	Men	Women	Age	BMI
2	Elise	Gill	92 Gloddaeth St	BIRCHAM TOFTS	PE31 0OR	08/04/81	166		62.4	31	
3	Chloe	Vincent	79 Essex Rd	TARBERT	HS2 4RC	09/04/78	156		50.6	34	
4	Andrew	Holland	63 Ivy Lane	WARDGATE	DE4 5II	04/12/72	187	87.3		39	25.0
5	Taylor	Bevan	59 Western Tce	MISERDEN	GL6 4OR	09/03/69	170	66.7		43	23.1
6	Kieran	Kirby	89 Sandyhill Rd	GAER	NP8 3FJ	11/08/49	179	109.5		62	34.2
7	Ellis	Holt	22 Circle Way	CAERAU	CF34 5YN	12/05/46	173	84		65	28.1
8	Tilly	North	46 Hindhead Rd	EARDINGTON	WV16 1CO	07/03/43	174		98.4	69	32.5
9	Faith	Bibi	25 Trinity Cr	WHEEDLEMON	AB54 8HC	01/06/42	170		59	69	20.4
10	Riley	Holt	52 Asfordby Rd	ALDBROUGH	DL11 5DL	02/11/40	188	112.1		71	31.7
11	Zachary	Vincent	58 Netherpark Cr	STETCHWORTH	CB8 0HZ	02/04/28	170	88.9		84	30.8

Sheet1

The drop-down menus above the document change to Calc ones when the spreadsheet opens. You'll be using the little black squares (circled) in Section 10.7.

Change cell *I1* to read *Weight* instead of *Men*. Select cells *J2* to *J11* and press CTRL+X to cut them. Click on cell *I2* and click *Edit > Paste Special....* A dialogue box appears. Make sure *Paste all* is ticked. Tick *Skip empty cells* under *Options*, then click OK . You may see a box asking whether to overwrite existing data. Click Yes . All the weights are now in column *I*.

If you'd just pasted cells J2 to J11 into column I, the empty cells (e.g. J2) would have overwritten the men's weights. Using Paste Special... and choosing to Skip empty cells avoided this.

Be sure to use cut rather than copy to start this operation: this ensures that references to the cells are changed to their new locations.

Click on the letter *J* above column *J* and click *Edit > Delete Cells....* The column disappears.

You can select several columns at once or select rows instead of columns and click Edit > Delete Cells... to get rid of them.

If you select a cell or range of cells that don't make up a whole row or column and click Edit > Delete Cells..., you'll see a dialogue box where you can choose whether to delete just the selected cells and move the cells in all rows below up to fill the space or move the cells in all columns to the right leftwards. You can also choose to delete the rows or columns containing the selected cells entirely.

If you want to delete the cell contents but leave the blank cells in place, you can press DELETE. If you press BACKSPACE instead, you'll be asked whether you want to delete everything in the cells or just certain elements such as text, numbers, formulas or formatting such as bold that you've applied to the cells.

Look at the X-Y chart you pasted in at the top of the page. It still shows men and women separately. The chart is just a copy. It's no longer linked to either People.ods or to the part of People.ods pasted separately into the Writer document. It won't update.

Click on cell *G11* and retype the date as *2/4/28*. Press RETURN. Mr. Vincent's age in cell *J3* is negative again. Press CTRL+Z to undo this change.

The embedded spreadsheet updates when you change data, just like the original one.

Click twice below the embedded spreadsheet. It closes: it's now just columns of text, etc.

The first time you click outside the spreadsheet, it shows green squares (handles) around it and an anchor symbol. You'll see how to use these later. The second click closes it completely.

What you learned:

- **How to see and quickly open LibreOffice documents you worked on recently.**
- **A situation where it's useful to have two programs running at the same time.**
- **How to paste charts from a spreadsheet into a Writer document.**
- **How to embed part of a spreadsheet into a Writer document.**

- **That you can edit the embedded spreadsheet just as if you were using Calc.**

- **That the embedded spreadsheet updates just as if you were using Calc.**

- **How** to use *Edit > Paste Special...* **to merge columns in a spreadsheet.**

- **How to delete a column from a spreadsheet.**

- **How to close an embedded spreadsheet.**

- *How to use ALT+TAB to switch between open documents.*

- *How to delete multiple columns or rows or a range of cells from a spreadsheet.*

- *How to selectively delete the contents of cells, leaving the cells themselves in place.*

- *That spreadsheet cells and charts pasted separately are no longer linked.*

10.2 Pasting tables and screenshots

Switch to the *People* spreadsheet. Check that cells *B1* to *L11* are still selected (highlighted). Press CTRL+C to copy them to the clipboard.

Switch to the new Writer document, click below the embedded spreadsheet and click *Edit > Paste Special...*. A dialogue box appears. Click to highlight *Formatted text [RTF]*. Click OK . The cells are pasted into the document again but this time as a simple table rather than an embedded spreadsheet.

> *Edit > Paste or CTRL+V pastes whatever is on the clipboard into your document with as much of its formatting and functionality as possible. Sometimes that's not what you want. Edit > Paste Special... shows you the different ways that the paste can be done and lets you choose. Unfortunately the names of the different choices can be obscure.*

> *You already encountered RTF (Rich Text Format) as a file format in Section 7.12. The formatting of the spreadsheet is kept but its functionality is lost.*

> *Another useful option under Paste Special is **Unformatted text**. This puts whatever is on the clipboard into the document as if you'd just typed it in, without keeping formatting such as its*

original font. For example, if you find some useful information on a web page and you want to paste it into a document that's already formatted, you don't want the pasted text to be in the web designer's choice of font.

Switch to the *People* spreadsheet. Hold down the ALT key and press the small key marked *Print Scrn*. It's usually near the top right of the keyboard and may have a slightly different label. A screenshot is made of the spreadsheet window and a dialogue box appears. Click Copy to Clipboard . The screenshot is put on the clipboard.

Pressing ALT+Print Scrn captures the current active window. Pressing Print Scrn on its own captures the whole screen, including all visible windows and the Launcher. As well as or instead of copying to the clipboard, the dialogue box lets you save the screenshot as a file.

Click Cancel . Switch to the new Writer document, click below the table and press CTRL+V. The screenshot is pasted into the document.

The screenshot is a picture: it's as if you'd used a digital camera to photograph your computer's screen. Instead of pasting, you could click Insert > Picture > From file... and choose any picture (e.g. a photograph) that's stored on your computer.

Instead of pasting the screenshot directly into your document, you could start a picture editing program such as GIMP (Section 12.1) and paste it there. Then you could make changes such as cropping it to remove bits you don't want or adding circles around things as you've seen in this book. You can then either save it as a file and use Insert > Picture > From file... or copy it back to the clipboard and paste it into your document.

Click on the screenshot and press BACKSPACE. You saw how to insert it but we don't want it.

Insert > Picture > From file... puts a copy of the picture into your document. Moving, changing or deleting the original file doesn't affect the copy. Removing the picture from the document deletes the copy but doesn't affect the original file.

Click on the table (not the embedded spreadsheet) and click *Table > Delete > Table*. The table disappears: we don't want that either.

If you tried to use BACKSPACE or DELETE to get rid of the table, it would only affect letters in it. Even if you select all the text in the table and press DELETE, the empty table remains.

What you learned:

- **How to paste spreadsheet cells into a Writer document as a table.**
- **How to copy a screenshot to the clipboard.**
- **How to paste a screenshot into a Writer document.**
- **How to remove a screenshot or picture from the document.**
- **How to delete a table in the document.**
- *How to paste text into your document without bringing along its formatting.*
- *How to insert a picture or photograph on your computer into the document.*
- *That inserting a picture or photograph makes a new copy that's part of the document.*
- *That you can edit screenshots or other pictures before you put them in your document.*

10.3 Formulas

Sometimes you might need to put a mathematical formula or equation into a document, e.g. $\dfrac{-b \pm \sqrt{b^2 - 4ac}}{2a}$. Click *Insert > Object >*

Formula. A LibreOffice Math formula object is inserted and you can type the formula into the box that appears below. E.g., the quadratic formula above can be typed in as *{-b+-sqrt{b^2-4 a c}} over {2 a}*. Click outside the box. Math automatically formats it. For more details, click *Help > LibreOffice Help* and look under *Formulas* on the *Contents* tab.

10.4 Portrait, Landscape and paper size

Click to the right of the column chart and confirm that the text cursor is between it and the embedded spreadsheet. Hold down CTRL and press RETURN. A page break is inserted.

The spreadsheet is now on a separate page but it's too wide to fit comfortably. We'd like the second page to use Landscape orientation.

Common paper sizes such as A4 (210 x 297 mm) and Letter (8½ x 11 inch) aren't square. Portrait orientation puts the shorter side at the top while landscape orientation puts the longer side there. Think of paintings of a person (**portrait**) or a scene (**landscape**) in an art gallery.

You don't need to change the way that the paper is loaded into the printer when you print a landscape page. The computer automatically rotates the image of the page when it sends it to the printer.

You can click Format > Page..., click the Page tab in the dialogue box and change the page size for your document. Usually, this should match the size of the paper loaded into the printer.

The **printer driver** installed in Ubuntu to control your particular printer needs to know the size of the paper. You can set this after clicking File > Print... by clicking Properties... next to the printer selection.

If the document page and printer paper sizes differ, your options depend on the printer driver and can't be covered in detail here. Possibilities include:

- Printing the page normal size with blank space or bits missing.

- Shrinking or enlarging the page to fit the paper.

- Printing each large page on several smaller sheets of paper that you stick together afterwards (**tiling**).

- Printing multiple pages on each sheet of paper, e.g. two A5 portrait pages side by side on an A4 landscape sheet.

- Showing an error message or flashing indicator light.

Your printer might be able to print on both sides of the paper (**duplex printing**). If not, you can print one side, reload the pages and print the other side but this always involves trial and error.

Press CTRL+Z to undo the page break. Click *Insert > Manual Break....* A dialogue box appears. Choose *Page break* as the *Type*, click ⇕ and select *Landscape* (you may need to scroll down in the list). Click

.

The embedded spreadsheet is now on a second page which is in Landscape orientation: it's wider than it is high.

Writer has predefined page styles: Landscape is one of these. As with paragraph styles, you can modify the predefined styles or add new ones.

If you insert another page break after Landscape pages, you can switch back to Portrait orientation the same way that you switched to Landscape by choosing Default as the Style.

What you learned:

- **How to start a new page by inserting a page break with CTRL+RETURN.**
- **How to change the orientation of pages from Portrait to Landscape.**
- *What Portrait and Landscape pages are.*
- *That Writer has predefined styles for pages as well as paragraphs.*
- *That you can modify these styles or add new ones.*
- *How to change subsequent pages back from Landscape to Portrait orientation.*
- *How to change page and paper sizes.*
- *What might happen if the sizes don't match.*
- *Two ways to print on both sides of the paper.*

10.5 Sizing and positioning graphics

Click on the X-Y chart of weight versus height that you pasted at the start of the document. You'll see small green squares at its corners and in the middle of each side. These are **handles**. Place the mouse cursor over the one at the middle of the bottom and drag it upwards. The chart gets shorter but it becomes squashed and looks wrong.

Press CTRL+Z to restore it. Try dragging the green square upwards again but this time hold down SHIFT while you do it. The chart shortens and gets narrower in proportion so that its shape is retained. Drag until the chart is just over half as high as it was originally.

You can drag the green square in the middle of any side to move that side inwards or outwards. You can drag a corner square to move the two adjacent sides.

Pressing SHIFT during any of these operations makes them retain the proportions.

The X-Y chart may disappear behind the column chart. We'll get it back in a bit.

Click on the column chart so the green square handles appear around it. Press SHIFT and drag any of the handles inwards until it too is just over half its original height. Right-click in the middle of the column chart, place the cursor over *Wrap*, then click on *Page Wrap*.

Put the mouse cursor in the middle of the chart and drag it to the left until its left side about lines up with the left-hand margin of the page.

You should now be able to see at least part of the X-Y chart. Click on it to select it.

Right-click in the middle of the X-Y chart, place the cursor over *Wrap*, then click on *Page Wrap*. Drag this chart to the right until its right side lines up with the right-hand margin of the page.

*Charts, pictures, drawings and embedded spreadsheets are all classed as graphics. **Wrapping** controls how text on the page appears around a graphic. The options are:*

- *No Wrap: the graphic has its own space on the page without any text alongside it.*

- *Page Wrap: text fits in alongside the graphic. It needs be placed on the left or right side. If you put it in the middle, you'll get text on both sides which isn't normally what you'd want.*

- *Optimal Page Wrap: this is the same as Page Wrap except that, if you put the graphic near the middle of the page (horizontally), text is put alongside on the wider side only.*

- *Wrap Through: Text is placed as if the graphic wasn't there, then the graphic is placed over the text. Text behind it is hidden unless the graphic has transparent areas.*

- *In Background: Text is placed as if the graphic wasn't there, then the graphic is placed behind it. This can be used to set a light-coloured logo or a word such as DRAFT as a background.*

If you tick First Paragraph, the wrapping option only applies to the first paragraph that lines up with the graphic. Later paragraphs are placed below it as if you'd selected No Wrap.

When you insert a graphic in your document, it has a rectangular shape but you may not want all of it to be included. For example, suppose you paste a triangular logo into your document. You want the text to wrap around the logo rather than around the whole rectangular graphic. Right-click the graphic and select Edit Contour....

The Contour Editor includes an auto-contour tool that works on the basis of colours. Closing the editor is tricky: the best way is to right-click the graphic again and clear the tick beside Edit Contour in the Wrap submenu.

If you right-click on a graphic and choose Object..., a dialogue box appears with many tabs. There are additional options on the Wrap tab. You can also set a border and background colour for the graphic.

The two charts may be overlapping. If so, click on the column chart and drag it down until it's below the X-Y chart.

Click at the top left of the page and type (pressing RETURN each time you see ¶):

What shape are you?¶
¶
I compared the height and weight of ten people. This chart shows what I found.¶
¶
The women are generally shorter although the taller women are taller than the shortest men.¶
¶
Taller people, both women and men, generally weigh more than shorter ones.¶
¶
This chart shows the age and Body Mass Index of the ten people.¶
¶
There's very little sign here that Body Mass Index varies with age.¶

Click on the column chart. You should have something similar to this:

What shape are you?

I compared the height and weight of ten people. This chart shows what I found.

The women are generally shorter although the taller women are taller than the shortest men.

Taller people, both women and men, generally weigh more than shorter ones.

This chart shows the age and Body Mass Index of the ten people.

There's very little sign here that Body Mass Index varies with age.

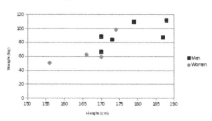

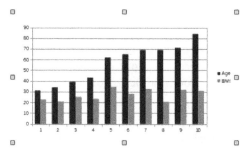

Depending exactly where you put the charts, it could be quite a bit different. Don't worry – it'll come out OK in the end.

What you learned:

- **How to change the size of a chart or other graphic.**
- **How to keep the height and width of a graphic in proportion when you resize it.**
- **How to set the text wrapping option so that text appears alongside a graphic.**
- **How to move a graphic from side to side on the page.**
- *What is meant by a "graphic".*
- *What the various options are for how text wraps around a graphic.*
- *How to make a smaller contour around your graphic.*

- *How to set a border and background colour for a graphic.*

10.6 Anchoring the graphics

Notice the **anchor** symbol (circled). This shows where the column chart is anchored. It may vary a bit.

Click on the X-Y chart. It also has an anchor symbol. Drag the X-Y chart itself. The anchor moves with it. Drag it upwards or downwards until the anchor is over *I compared*.

Click on *What shape are you?*. Select *Heading 1* from the paragraph style list and click 🔲. The heading is centred. Note that part of it extends over the X-Y chart.

Click on the column chart and drag it upwards or downwards until its anchor lines up with *This chart shows the age*.

Click just before the start of the line that starts *Taller people* and press RETURN. The line moves downwards. So do the following lines and the column chart.

> *The column chart is anchored to This chart and moves with it. I compared and the X-Y chart that's anchored to it don't move.*

Keep pressing RETURN until the *Taller people* line is below the X-Y chart and widens out.

You might need to make minor adjustments such as dragging the charts sideways to line up correctly with the text margins and adding another blank line after *shorter ones*. Page 1 should now look good.

What shape are you?

I compared the height and weight of ten people. This chart shows what I found.

The women are generally shorter although the taller women are taller than the shortest men.

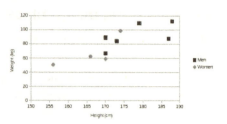

Taller people, both women and men, generally weigh more than shorter ones.

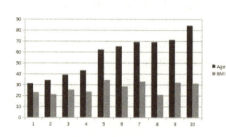

This chart shows the age and Body Mass Index of the ten people.

There's very little sign here that Body Mass Index varies with age.

When you insert a chart, picture or other graphic, it's set to be anchored To Paragraph. If you right-click on a chart or other graphic and place the cursor over Anchor, you'll see other options. You can anchor the graphic to the page so it stays in the same place whatever you do to the text.

You can anchor it as a character. This is quite different. The graphic is like a character in the text (rather than being somewhere to the side of it). If the graphic is higher than other characters in the line of text, the spacing of the lines increases to allow it to fit.

Small graphics such as 🏁 start *can be anchored as characters. Larger graphics can also be anchored as characters in paragraphs of their own.*

The anchor symbol isn't needed and you'll notice it disappears if you choose anchoring To Page or As Character. Anchoring To Character is only useful in a few situations.

Setting up the anchoring pays off when you make changes to your document.

What you learned:

- **How to move graphics up and down the page.**
- **What anchoring is.**
- **How to anchor a graphic to a specific paragraph so it stays with it when you make changes.**
- *How to anchor a graphic so it always stays in the same place on the page.*
- *How to anchor a graphic so it sits in your text just like a character.*

10.7 Adjusting the embedded spreadsheet

Click below the embedded spreadsheet on page 2. Press RETURN repeatedly until the text cursor is below the spreadsheet. Type:

The 10 people

Select the *Heading 1* paragraph style and click ▣.

Click on the spreadsheet and drag it down until it's below *The 10 people*.

When you start to drag, the cursor may change to a circle with a diagonal line indicating that the operation isn't permitted. It's a bit temperamental. Release the mouse button and try again with the cursor in a slightly different place over the spreadsheet.

You may have trouble seeing all of the embedded spreadsheet. Click *View > Zoom....* A dialogue box opens. Select *Fit width* and click OK .

There are other zoom options. For example, you can choose to see the entire page at once but the text will probably be too small to read.

Click on the embedded spreadsheet, then click ▣. Double-click the spreadsheet to open it.

Use the spreadsheet scrollbars (arrowed in the Section 10.1 screenshot) to put the top left cell that needs to be visible in the top left of the window. It's cell B1 in this case. Drag the black square handles (two of them are circled in the screenshot) to resize the window so you can see all the cells that you want to be visible without unwanted blank rows or columns.

The embedded spreadsheet can be any size but only the cells that are visible in the window when it's open will be visible in the document when it's closed.

Click outside the spreadsheet to close it. Now page 2 is the way we want it.

Close the new document. You won't be using it again but you can save it for posterity if you want. You can also close the *People* spreadsheet, discarding any changes.

What you learned:

- **Another way to zoom to see more or less of the page at a time on the screen.**

- **How to choose which cells in an embedded spreadsheet are visible.**

11 Frames, drawing and columns

If you need to lay out a magazine or newspaper, you can use a desktop publishing (DTP) program. You can easily install Scribus (see Section 12.1) and try it out. Professional publishers use very powerful and expensive DTP programs.

LibreOffice has DTP capabilities too. This chapter shows how to use it to make a simple newsletter. It also uses LibreOffice Draw to create and embed a simple logo.

11.1 Making a frame with columns

Start LibreOffice Writer. A new document opens.

Click *Insert > Frame...*. A dialogue box opens. Click the *Borders* tab and, under *Line arrangement*, click ☐ (its tooltip says *Set No Borders*). Click the *Columns* tab and choose 2 columns (set the box to 2 or click on the two-column layout). Set the *Spacing* box to *0.8* cm (or *0.3* in). Click ⎡ OK ⎤. A small box with 8 green handles appears. This is going to be the main frame for the newsletter.

> *The frame will contain text in two columns 0.8 cm apart, a drawing and another frame and you'll see how they interact. It's also possible to set up columns on the page itself using Format > Page....*

Click ▤. The box moves to the left side of the page. Drag the middle green handle on the right side rightwards to the right margin. Click outside the box. The handles disappear.

Open *LazyDog* (the first word-processor document you made). Click in it, press CTRL+A, then press CTRL+C. All the text is copied to the clipboard.

> *In Chapter 10 you had a Writer document and a Calc spreadsheet open at the same time. Now, you have two Writer documents open at once. You can use the LibreOffice Window menu to switch between them.*
>
> *Alternatively, click 📑 on the Launcher. You'll see both Writer documents in miniature. Click on the one you want.*

You can use ALT+TAB too. When LibreOffice Writer is highlighted in the box, continue holding down ALT. After a short delay, the open Writer documents appear. Press TAB again to move the outline around the one you want, then release ALT.

Go back to the new document, click in the frame and press CTRL+V. The drivel about the fox and the dog is pasted in two columns.

What you learned:

- **How to create a frame.**
- **How to change the width of a frame.**
- **How to set up columns.**
- *How to use the Launcher or ALT+TAB to switch between documents associated with the same program.*

11.2 Making a logo

This uses LibreOffice Draw to create a new logo. If you had a logo as a file on your computer, you could use Insert > Picture > From File... as discussed in Section 10.2.

Click just before the first word (*The*) in the two columns. Click *Insert > Object > OLE Object...*. A dialogue box opens. Choose *LibreOffice Drawing* and click OK . An embedded drawing appears. The menus and toolbars change to those needed to work on the drawing. There's a drawing toolbar below the document.

*⊳ chooses a tool that lets you select, move and resize objects in your drawing such as a text block, a line or a shape. **T** chooses a tool that lets you type text into your drawing. ⬭ chooses a tool that creates ellipses and circles. There are other tools to create polygons including squares and to draw lines. These aren't covered here.*

*Computers work with two different types of pictures and drawings. A **bit-mapped** picture specifies the brightness and colour of each point in it. It can show anything: photographs are always bit-mapped. If you try to enlarge a bit-map too much, its individual points become visible as squares and it looks bad.*

*A **vector graphic** contains instructions to draw shapes, colour them in and overlay them. It's limited in what it can show but has* *the advantage that you can easily move and change individual shapes and you can enlarge the graphic to any size.*

GIMP works with bit-mapped pictures. LibreOffice Draw works with vector graphics and you can install the more powerful Inkscape (see Section 12.1). These aren't covered in detail here but you can experiment...

*OLE stands for Object Linking and Embedding. An **embedded object** (e.g. our drawing) is part of the document and is saved in its file. You can choose to **link** to an external file instead. For example you could record sales in a spreadsheet and prepare several different reports linked to that spreadsheet file. Updating the spreadsheet updates all the reports too but if you e-mail a report file to someone else, you need to send the spreadsheet file as well.*

You can use Insert > Object > OLE Object... to embed a new spreadsheet too and, of course, this can look like a list or table in the document. This could be handy if, for example, you're preparing an invoice. Let the spreadsheet do the arithmetic.

Click **T** on the drawing toolbar, then click in the embedded drawing. Type *Sunnyside News.*

Right-click on the edge of the box surrounding *Sunnyside News* and click on *Fontwork.* A dialogue box appears:

Set the three circled options and click ⊗ to close the dialogue box. *Sunnyside News* is now in an arc with a shadow effect.

If you're using inches, set the shadow distance to 0.04.

Click ⬭ on the drawing toolbar. Place the cursor under *Sunnyside News*, hold down SHIFT and drag to create a circle the right size to fit under the words. Right-click on the circle, choose *Area...* and select *Yellow* (near the top of the list in the dialogue box). Click OK . The circle now contains a yellow colour.

Right-click on the circle again and choose *Line....* Click the *Line* tab and select *Style* as *Invisible* (at the top of the list in the dialogue box). Click OK . The circle no longer has a dark line around it.

*Vector graphic shapes have a **fill** and a **stroke** although LibreOffice Draw doesn't use these terms. The fill is the colour inside the shape while the stroke is the line around it. You've set the fill to Yellow and made the stroke invisible. Sometimes you may want to set the fill to none and just use the stroke. Sometimes, you'll want to use both.*

Place the cursor over the circle and drag it until it fits as well as possible under the words.

Click to place the cursor above and to the left of the words and circle. Drag down to the right. The outline of a box appears. Keep dragging until both the words and the circle are inside the box.

Right-click on the circle. Choose *Alignment* and click *Centered*. The circle is now centred exactly under the words.

Right-click on the circle. Click *Group*.

*The circle and words are now **grouped** so they can be resized or moved together easily. If you ever need to separate them again, right-click and choose Ungroup.*

Click on the circle and drag it and the words up to the top left of the drawing, ignoring the page outline and margins.

The drawing window has little black squares around it like the embedded spreadsheet did (Section 10.7). Use the one at the bottom right corner to resize it so that the new logo is all visible with a minimum of blank space around it.

Click outside the drawing window. It closes. Drag the logo up to the top of the left-hand column.

What you learned:

- **That you can create an embedded drawing using LibreOffice Draw.**
- **How to do a few things in Draw.**
- **How to choose which parts of the drawing are visible.**
- **How to anchor a graphic to a frame.**
- *The differences between bit-mapped and vector graphics.*
- *What Fill and Stroke (Line) are.*
- *What an object is.*
- *The differences between linking and embedding an object.*
- *Uses for linked and embedded spreadsheets.*

11.3 Overlapping frames

Click just before the first word (*The*) in the two columns again. Click *Insert > Frame*. The *Frame* dialogue box appears again. Click the *Borders* tab. Click ▣ (*Cast Shadow to Bottom Right*) under *Shadow style*. Click the *Background* tab and choose *Light green* as the *Background color*. Click ▣ OK ▣. A new frame with a green background and shadow effect appears.

Type *April 2012*. It appears in the frame. Drag to select *April 2012* and change it to *Liberation Sans 18pt Bold*. Click ▣ to centre it.

Click on the edge of the frame. The handles appear. Drag the box to cover the bottom of the yellow circle in the logo. Use the green handles to make it as wide as the logo and move its bottom up so *April 2012* just fits nicely.

> *You can right-click on the frame, choose Arrange and click Send to Back to put the frame behind the yellow circle.*
>
> *Right-click on the yellow circle, choose Arrange again and click Send to Back. The logo moves behind the frame you can see April 2012 again.*
>
> *If you have more than two overlapping frames, you can use Bring Forward and Send Backward to stack them in front of one another in any order you want.*

If you need to delete a frame, click on its edge so that the handles appear, then press DELETE.

What you learned:

- **How to create a frame with a border, background colour and shadow effect.**
- **That you can type text into a frame and format it.**
- *What happens when frames overlap.*
- *How to use the different Arrange options.*
- *How to delete a frame.*

11.4 Linking frames

Click at the bottom of the page below the two columns. Click *Insert > Frame*. The *Frame* dialogue box appears. Click on the *Borders* tab and click ☐ (*Set No Borders*) under *Line arrangement*. Click OK . A new small frame with handles appears at the top of the page. Drag it down below the two columns, and click ▤. Drag the middle green handle on the right side rightwards to the right margin.

Click on the edge of one of the two columns above. Frame handles appear around the columns. Click ⚏ (the tool-tip says *Link Frames*) in the toolbar above the ruler. Click in the new frame under the two columns. A dotted line appears between the right-hand column and the new frame. They are now linked.

Drag the handle at the bottom middle of the two columns upwards. The text no longer fits in the columns. What won't fit there appears in the new frame underneath. Adjust the handle until *What do these dogs like?* is the first text in the new frame.

> *The text flows from the first frame into the linked frame. Changes you make to the first frame or the text in it affects how much text flows into the linked frame.*
>
> *You can repeat the linking process to link another frame to the last linked frame.*
>
> *If you were laying out a newspaper, you could use a linked frame to continue a front page story on an inside page.*

Click on the edge of the new frame, then drag it upwards until it looks reasonable.

April 2012

The quick brown fox jumps over a lazy dog. **The quick brown fox jumps over a lazy dog.** *The quick brown fox jumps over a lazy dog.* The quick brown fox jumps over the lazy dog. ***The quick brown fox jumps over the lazy dog.***

jumps over a lazy dog. **The quick brown fox jumps over a lazy dog.** *The quick brown fox jumps over a lazy dog.* The quick brown fox jumps over the lazy dog. ***The quick brown fox jumps over the lazy dog.***

The quick brown fox jumps over a lazy dog. **The quick brown fox jumps over a lazy dog.** *The quick brown fox jumps over a lazy dog.* The quick brown fox jumps over the lazy dog. **The quick brown fox jumps over the lazy dog.**

The quick brown fox

What do these dogs like? Walkies Chasing things Barking Eating Sleeping

Close the new document. You won't be using it again but you can save it for posterity if you want.

What you learned:

- **How to link frames so that text flows between them.**
- **How to make a page look right by dragging frames.**
- *That newspapers are laid out with linked frames to continue stories on other pages.*

11.5 Making a letterhead

Now that you've seen how to import graphics and set up a page with frames, you can design your own letterhead.

You can put a logo at the top. Perhaps you already have one that you can insert as a graphic or you could try designing one with Draw.

You can put contact details in a frame at the top or bottom of the page.

When you're happy with the design, save it as a Writer template (Section 7.13). No need to have the letterhead printed, just open the template whenever you start writing a letter.

You need to weigh up the advantages and disadvantages of doing this. A letterhead printed with each letter will print more slowly, will probably be lower quality and may cost more in ink or toner. On the other hand, you'll be sure your letters line up with the letterhead, you won't have to change paper in the printer, there won't be a minimum print run and you can change details on the letterhead (e.g. your phone number) at any time.

12 Advanced Ubuntu

If you have problems with Windows, you can usually find a friend who knows how to sort them out.

Ubuntu is more reliable and it's often easier to sort out if something is wrong but it's harder to find someone knowledgeable to help you with it. This chapter aims to give you the basic knowledge you need to do things yourself.

12.1 Installing more programs

Programs such as clamav, GIMP, Inkscape and Scribus have already been mentioned. They probably won't be installed yet on your computer but it's very easy to add them.

Click ⬛ on the Launcher. **Ubuntu Software Center** starts after a few seconds. There are various ways to browse for programs but it's usually easiest to use the search box at the top right.

Type *gnome-system* into the box. A list of programs appears. Look for *gnome-system-tools* in the list – you might have to scroll down to see it.

You'll use gnome-system-tools in Section 12.9.

Click on it and click ⬛Install⬛. You're asked for your password. Type it in and press RETURN or click ⬛Authenticate⬛. The program is downloaded from the Ubuntu software repository and is installed on your computer. This may take a few minutes.

Once it's installed, you see ⬛Remove⬛ in place of ⬛Install⬛. At any time, you can start the Ubuntu Software Center, find a program that you've installed previously and click ⬛Remove⬛ to remove it from your computer.

Type *base* into the search box. *LibreOffice Base* should appear in the list. Click on it and click ⬛Install⬛. Again, you'll be asked for your password. The program is downloaded and installed.

A new icon (⬛) appears on the Launcher. This is discussed in Section 12.2. You'll need LibreOffice Base in Chapter 13.

Type *restricted* into the search box. *Ubuntu restricted extras* should appear in the list. Click on it and click [More Info]. You see a description.

> *This is a package of programs which allow your computer to do various things such as creating and playing MP3 music files. It can also install some Windows fonts including Arial and Times New Roman (Section 5.11). Depending where you live, it might not be completely legal for you to install some of the programs so they aren't included as standard in Ubuntu. If you decide you want to install the package, click [Install]. You can tick a box to accept the Microsoft True Type core fonts End User License Agreement (EULA) and install the fonts (see Section 12.4), then click [Forward].*

> *Commercial video DVDs are encrypted. They can be played on Ubuntu but there are even more legal complexities. Type ubuntu libdvdcss into a search engine to find out more.*

> *You can type a program name or a word or words from its description into the search box. Program names such as GIMP are bandied around but you'll often need to look at the description to find out what they do.*

Click (x) to close the Ubuntu Software Center.

What you learned:

- **How to use the Ubuntu Software Center to quickly and easily find and install programs.**
- *That there are legal and licensing issues preventing some programs and fonts being included in Ubuntu.*
- *That you can often install these yourself.*
- *How to use the Ubuntu Software Center to remove programs.*

12.2 Tweaking the Launcher

> *You'll have noticed that the Launcher takes up valuable screen space. You can change this.*

Click at the top right of the screen, then click *System Settings...*. The *System Settings* box appears. Click *Appearance* under *Personal*.

Click the *Look* tab. At the bottom, there's a *Launcher icon size* slider. Sliding this to the left makes the Launcher narrower. You see the effect immediately. You might like to reduce it from the default size of 48 to around 35.

Click on the *Behavior* tab. If you change the switch on the right hand side from OFF to ON, the Launcher disappears entirely (*Auto-hide*). It reappears when you move the mouse cursor all the way to the left side of the screen.

> *When you switch Auto-hide on, you may find that the Launcher is occasionally shy about reappearing and the Reveal sensitivity slider has little or no effect. You might end up switching Auto-hide off again.*

As mentioned in Section 12.1, new icons may appear on the Launcher when you install programs. There may be some icons that were already there that you never use. To get rid of an unwanted icon, right-click on it and click *Unlock from Launcher*.

> *Section 12.9 shows how to start a program that doesn't have a Launcher icon and how to add or restore its icon to the Launcher.*

What you learned:

- **How to change the Launcher icon size.**
- **How to auto-hide the Launcher.**
- **How to remove unwanted icons from the Launcher.**

12.3 Changing the way to open files and folders.

As mentioned in Section 6.1, Nautilus can be set to use either of two methods to open folders and files:

- With the first method, clicking selects a folder or file and double-clicking opens it.
- With the second method, a single click opens a folder or file.

You can change the method by starting Nautilus and clicking *Edit > Preferences*. A dialogue box opens. Click on the *Behavior* tab and click the radio button under *Behavior* for the method you prefer.

Ubuntu doesn't have the hover select method you might know from Windows. If you choose to open folders and files with a single click, you can use any of these methods when you need to select a folder or file without opening it:

- Hold down CTRL and click on it.

- In Icon view, drag over its icon to create a marquee (Section 6.6).

- In List view, click just to the left of its icon.

12.4 Adding Windows fonts

If you installed Ubuntu Restricted Extras and accepted the Microsoft EULA (Section 12.1), you'll already be able to use some Windows fonts such as Arial and Times New Roman.

If you chose not to install them then or if there are other fonts in Windows that you'd like to use, you can follow this section.

Click ▢ on the Launcher to start Nautilus. As in Section 6.5, click on your Windows disk drive to open it.

Remember you might have to click ⏚ File System, then click the host folder instead.

Open the *Windows* (or WINDOWS) folder. Open the *Fonts* folder.

You see all the fonts that are installed in Windows. If you click or double click on any of them, the *Font Viewer* starts. Clicking on Install Font adds the font to your Ubuntu system, e.g. so you can use it in Writer.

12.5 Adding LibreOffice extensions

As well as additional dictionaries (Section 5.13), you can add LibreOffice extensions to do other useful things.

Click ▣ on the Launcher. Once Writer starts, click *Tools > Extension Manager...*.

A dialogue box appears. Click *Get more extensions online...* near the bottom left. Firefox starts and opens the *LibreOffice Extensions* page.

By the time you read this, the page may have changed. Currently, you can click *Extensions* on the bar near the top, then browse the available extensions. If you want to install a dictionary (Section 5.13), click the *Dictionaries of different languages* category on the right hand side.

Once you see the extension you want in Firefox, click on it. You're taken to a page with more details about the extension. These pages vary quite a bit – you may see the file you want there or you might have to do some more clicking to get to it.

What you're looking to do is to download a file whose name ends with .oxt. You can see the file name at the bottom of the Firefox window when the mouse pointer is over the link. In the case of the British and Canadian dictionaries, different versions are listed on the project page and you can click on the one you want.

Instead of navigating through the LibreOffice site, it might be easier to use a search engine such as Google to track down the extension you want. All you're trying to do is to find the .oxt file. Be suspicious if the file location as shown at the bottom of the Firefox window isn't on the libreoffice.org site. The file might contain malware.

After you click on the link, choose *Save File* in the dialogue box that appears and click [OK]. The file is downloaded – this might take a while.

You can close Firefox now if you want to. Switch back to the *LibreOffice Extension Manager* dialogue box (e.g. using ALT+TAB) and click [Add]. The *Add Extension* dialogue box opens.

You may see the *.oxt* file you just downloaded. If not, click the *Downloads* folder at the left side. Once you see the *.oxt* file, click to select it then click [Open].

Perhaps after a delay, the new extension appears in the *Extension Manager* dialogue box. It may not actually work until you close and restart Writer.

After you install a dictionary, click Tools > Options. The Options dialogue box appears. Click ▶ to the left of Language Settings on the left hand side, then click Languages. ᴬᴮᶜ should now appear alongside your language under Default languages for documents. Make sure the language is selected and click [OK].

If you click Tools > Extension Manager..., then click on an extension that's listed, you'll see buttons to disable or completely remove it.

What you learned:

- **How to find and install LibreOffice extensions, including dictionaries for other languages.**

- *To be careful: an extension might contain malware.*

- *How to disable or completely remove an extension.*

12.6 Drivers

When you buy equipment such as a printer or scanner, it usually includes a disk. You use this to install programs that a Windows or Apple computer uses to control the equipment: these programs are known as **drivers**.

> *When you follow the instructions to install the drivers, you'll often find that a lot of other programs that you didn't want have also been installed. These are colloquially known as **crapware**.*

It's extremely rare to find Linux drivers included on the disks. This is partly because there aren't that many Linux users and it's also because there are too many different Linux distributions. Instead, you'll find that your new equipment falls into one of the following categories:

- The Linux kernel already knows about it and has the drivers. You connect the equipment (e.g. with a USB cable) and it just works – so much easier than with Windows. You might have to change some settings, e.g. enter a password for a wireless network.

- You can get the equipment working by putting its make, model and *Linux* into a search engine and following tips that turn up. They might say how to find, download and install the driver you need.

- The equipment isn't supported at all. Some functions might still work, e.g. a stylus may work as a mouse but not be pressure-sensitive.

Most equipment from well known manufacturers falls into the first category but there's often something you want to use that doesn't. It's a good idea to use a search engine to see if equipment you're interested in will work with Ubuntu before you actually buy it.

What you learned:

- **If you're lucky, equipment such as a printer or scanner will just work once you plug it in.**

- **If you're unlucky, it won't. You might be able to fix it but it won't be easy.**

- **You should check if something you're interested in will work without too much trouble before you buy it.**

- *What crapware is and that it's mainly a problem with Windows.*

12.7 Configuring your printer

If the printer is connected directly to your computer with a cable, it should have been recognised and automatically set up the first time it was turned on. You'll have been able to use it as described in Section 5.15.

If this didn't happen, see below and Section 12.6.

Even when the printer is recognised and working, there may be settings that you want to adjust.

Click ⚙ at the top right of the screen, then click *Printers....* A window showing your printers appears. There might not be any.

If you see your printer, you can right click on it, then click on *Proper-ties*. The Printer Properties dialogue box appears. If you click *Settings* on the left hand side, you can change the printer name, etc. print a test page or perhaps do maintenance such as cleaning the print head. You can click other items such as *Printer Options* on the left hand side and change settings such as the default paper size. The options vary depending on the model of the printer.

If your printer doesn't appear, click ⊞ Add. The next dialogue box lets you set up a network printer or one that's being shared over the network by another (e.g. Windows) computer.

You can also add and administer printers by stating Firefox and typing localhost:631 into the address box. This connects you to the CUPS (Common Unix Printing System) server on your computer. It's more comprehensive and you might find it easier to understand. You may be asked to type in your user name and password before you can make changes.

12.8 Updates

As mentioned in Section 2.6, it's important to keep programs on your computer updated so that bugs are fixed and they are less vulnerable to malware.

Ubuntu automatically checks for updates every day. When they are available, █ appears on the launcher (it may show how many updates there are).

At a convenient time, click on it. The **Update Manager** starts and shows details about the updates.

At the time of writing, there's a bug and Update Manager may not start. Section 12.12 shows how to get it going.

Click `Install Updates`. The updates are downloaded and installed. This might take several minutes.

You can choose not to apply (install) some of the updates but it's hard to know which ones and why. You should trust Ubuntu and just apply them all.

Some updates require the computer to be restarted before they take effect. If so, you'll see a message and ⚙ at the top right of the screen turns red.

You don't have to restart right away: you can wait for a convenient time. Maybe you're planning to shut the computer down soon: the updates will take effect next time you start it up.

Ubuntu updating works much better than the Windows equivalent. It updates your application programs as well as Ubuntu itself, it doesn't impose itself when you have important work to do and it never restarts unexpectedly.

What you learned:

- **That Ubuntu automatically checks for updates, both to itself and to other installed programs.**
- **How to know when there are updates.**
- **How to install them.**
- **That you can choose when to install updates and, if a restart is needed, when to do it.**
- *That Windows updating is a pain but Ubuntu is much better.*

12.9 Users and permissions

Like most operating systems, Ubuntu lets you set up more than one user for your computer. Each user has a different name and password and has their own home folder where they keep their files.

Click ⊙ on the Launcher and type *users* into the search box. Click on *Users and Groups*.

Users and Groups is part of gnome-system-tools that you installed in Section 12.1. User Accounts (which can also be accessed from the System Settings box) is the standard Ubuntu tool but it's much more limited in what it can do.

You might have unlocked the icons for some installed programs so they no longer appear on the Launcher (Section 12.2). You can find and start any program by clicking ⊙ and typing either the start of its name or words from its description into the search box. You can also find document files on the computer by typing their name (or at least the first part of it) into the search box.

You can also open any recently used document (including ones not associated with LibreOffice) by clicking ⊙, then clicking the ☐ lens at the bottom of the screen. The recent documents are shown. Click on any of them to open it.

Once Users and Groups starts, its icon (👥) appears on the Launcher. It'll disappear again when you close Users and Groups. If you want to keep a program's icon there permanently, you can right-click on it and click Lock to Launcher.

You see the Ubuntu users currently set up on your computer. There will probably only be one: you. Click Add . You'll be asked for your password, then type in the full name of another user and a user name for them.

You'll need a second user to do some of the following steps. The user's full name is shown when logging in, etc.

Click OK . You're now asked to type in a password for them (twice). Do this and click OK .

You can tick Don't ask for password on login but they may still need to enter their password to unlock encrypted information such as a wireless network passphrase.

Click your name just to the left of ⚙ at the top right of the screen. You see a list of users. Click on the name of the one you just created and type in their password. You're now logged in as the new user.

You'll notice that the Launcher is back to how it was originally. Each user has their own preference settings. The new user can repeat Section 12.2, adjusting things to their own taste.

Click 📁 on the Launcher. Nautilus starts. Click ◿ File System and open *home*. It now contains a home folder for each user.

Open your own home folder (not that of the new user). Open *Documents*, then *WP files*. Open *LazyDog.odt*. It opens but is shown as read-only on the titlebar. Close it and close Nautilus.

Click the name to the left of ⚙ and switch to your own session.

Click 📁 on the Launcher to start Nautilus, click 🏠 Home on the left side, then right-click *Documents* in the main list of files and folders.

Click *Properties* in the list. A dialogue box appears. Click the *Permissions* tab (circled below).

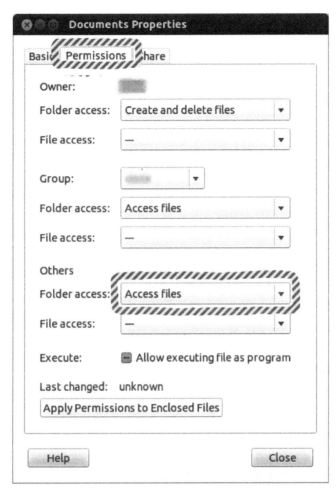

This shows who is allowed to do what with files and folders in your *Documents* folder. You, of course, are allowed to create and delete files as well as looking at what's in them.

Other users are allowed to access (look at) your documents but they can't change or delete them. Click ▾ to the right of *Folder access* (circled). Click *None* in the list that appears.

There are also permissions for a group (just above the circled part). Make sure its *Folder access* permission is set to *Access files*. Click ⌈Apply Permissions to Enclosed Files⌋. Click ⌈ Close ⌋.

> *You can also choose which group the folder belongs to: for now it should be the same as your user name. We'll look at groups in the next section.*

Click your name to the left of ⚙ and switch to the new user's session.

Click 🗀 on the Launcher to start Nautilus. Click ⬦ File System, open *home* and open your own home folder (not that of the new user).

Click or double-click on *Documents*. You now get an error message: the other user can no longer see any of your documents.

Click OK. Close Nautilus. Click ⚙, click *System Settings...* and click *User Accounts* under *System* in the window that appears. The User Accounts window opens with the new user's name highlighted.

Click in the *Password* box. A dialogue box opens. You could type in the new user's current password, then type in a new password twice and click Change.

A user can change their own password any time they like.

Instead, click Cancel. Click your own name and click the *Password* box. You see a message that you must click 🔒 Unlock first.

You're logged in as the new user: they can't make changes to any other user's account.

Click 🔒 Unlock. You're asked for your own password. Click Cancel, then close the User Accounts window.

When you installed Ubuntu, your account was set up as an Administrator. Once you've proved who you are by typing in your password, you can make changes to other users' accounts.

Click ⚙ and click *Log Out....* Click Log Out. The new user's session ends and you see a list of all users. Click on your own name and type in your password. You're back in your own user session.

What you learned:

- **How to start a program that doesn't have an icon on the Launcher.**
- **How to lock a program's icon so it's is always on the Launcher.**
- **How to add a user and set their password.**
- **How to log in as a different user.**
- **That each user has their own home folder and preferences.**

- **How to set permissions for your folders and files.**

- **How these permissions affect other users.**

- **That several users' accounts can be open at once.**

- **How to switch between them (so long as you know the passwords).**

- **How a user can change their own password.**

- **That you as an administrator can change other users' passwords and account details.**

- **How to log out of an account without shutting down the computer.**

- *That a user can be allowed to log in without using a password.*

- *That this isn't as useful as it might seem.*

- *How to find a document file when you've forgotten where you saved it.*

- *How to see and open any recently-used document.*

12.10 Groups

Groups are a powerful tool that lets you control which other users have access to your files.

Click 🔵 on the Launcher and type *users* into the search box. Click on *Users and Groups*. Click on ⬜ Manage Groups in the Users Settings window that appears.

You see a long list of groups, mostly with mysterious names

Ubuntu automatically creates a group for each user. You can click ⬜ Add *to create a new group.*

You must use Users and Groups rather than User Accounts when you want to manage groups.

Scroll down to find the group with your own user name. Click on it and click Properties .

A dialogue box appears. All the Ubuntu users are listed under *Group Members*. Click the tickbox to the left of the name of the user you added in Section 12.9 so that it's ticked. Click ⬜ OK , then click

| Close | twice to close the two windows.

The new user is now a member of your group.

Click your name to the left of [icon] and log in as the new user.

Click [icon] on the Launcher to start Nautilus. Click [icon] File System, open *home* and open your own home folder (not that of the new user).

Click or double-click on *Documents*. Now that they are a member of your group, the other user can open the folder.

> *A file or folder always belongs to a particular user (the owner) and one particular group. A user can be a member of many groups. If they are a member of the group that the file or folder belongs to, it's the group permissions for the file or folder that apply to them rather than the permissions for other users.*

> *Usually, you'll set the permissions for the group to allow them to do more than other users. You as the owner may be allowed to do even more again. You can set the permissions so that the owner or the group has fewer permissions but that isn't likely to be useful.*

> *Suppose you and several colleagues are working on a project. You make a new folder in your home folder to contain files relating to it. Your colleagues do the same. You want to allow your colleagues to look at and make changes to files in that folder and you want to be able to look in their similar folders too . but none of you want to allow the others to see all your documents.*

> *You do this by creating a new group for the project, making you and your colleagues members of the group, then setting all the relevant folders to that new group. You'll all need to remember to back up the folders separately since they aren't in Documents.*

What you learned:

- **That Ubuntu automatically sets up a group for each user.**
- **How to add users to a group.**
- **That, once a user is a member of a group, different permissions apply when they try to access a file or folder belonging to that group.**
- *That you can't use User Accounts to manage groups.*

- *How to create a new group.*

- *That a user can be a member of many groups and a group can have many users as its members.*

- *That a file or folder always belongs to a single group.*

- *How to create a new group that lets certain users access selected files.*

12.11 The command line

Click 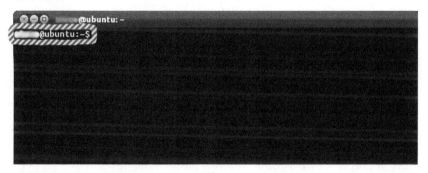 on the Launcher and type *term* into the search box. Click on *Terminal*.

The Terminal displays a command line prompt (circled). It shows your user name (blurred out here) and which folder on the system you're in (~ represents your home folder). You can directly type in Linux commands.

> *Ubuntu provides the Launcher and various graphical tools such as the Software Center but, underneath, it's a fairly standard Debian version of Linux. There are three main situations where you might want to use the command line:*
>
> - *You might want to use a program that only exists in a command line version (e.g. shred).*
>
> - *You might have used a search engine to find a fix for some problem but the instructions you find expect you to use the command line. This is because command line instructions are easy to describe and are much the same in all versions of Linux - even in other related versions of Unix such as Apple's OS-X.*

- *Often the command line is just quicker and easier. If you start to use it a lot, you can install and try the Midnight Commander command line file manager program.*

Click in the Terminal window. A rectangular cursor appears after the prompt. Type *ping google.com* and press RETURN. After a short delay, you should see a message starting with *64 bytes from google.com*. The message keeps repeating. Press CTRL+C. The ping program stops and the prompt appears again.

The message shows that your computer is able to see and communicate over the internet with the google.com server. You might be asked to use ping when someone is helping you to find out why you can't use a network connection.

Pressing CTRL+C usually forces a command line program to quit. If you want to copy text from the Terminal window, drag over it to highlight it, then use Edit > Copy instead of CTRL+C.

Type *cd ~/Documents/"WP files"* and press RETURN.

This moves to your *WP files* folder and the prompt changes to show this. You need to use the double quote marks because of the space in *WP files*.

Type *ls* and press RETURN. The *ls* program runs. It lists the files in the *WP files* directory, then exits. The prompt appears again.

ls (list) is a program that lists files in a directory.

Windows has a command line too and some of its commands are the same as the Linux ones. cd and ping are two of them but ls isn't: the equivalent in Windows is dir. Windows also traditionally uses a backslash to separate directories (e.g. Documents\WP files) but newer versions accept a forward slash too.

Type *cp LazyDog.odt xyz123.odt* and press RETURN. The *LazyDog.odt* file is copied to a new file called *xyz123.odt*.

The cp command expects to find LazyDog.odt in the current folder (the one showing in the prompt) and it makes the copy in the same folder. If you'd been in a different folder, you could have typed cp ~/Documents/"WP files"/LazyDog.odt xyz123.odt to put the copy in the other folder.

Type *lowriter xyz* (don't press RETURN). Press TAB. The line changes to *lowriter xyz123.odt*.

Some file names can be extraordinarily long. When you press TAB, the file name is automatically completed for you. For this to work, there must only be one file name starting with the letters you've typed (xyz in this case).

Press RETURN. LibreOffice Writer starts and displays the document.

You can start a graphical program such as Writer from the command line.

Close Writer. Type *shred xyz123.odt* (of course you can use TAB completion again). Press RETURN.

Press the up arrow key. The previous command reappears. Press it again. The command before that appears *(lowriter xyz123.odt)*. Press RETURN.

The up and down arrow keys move through the list of previous commands. When you see the one you want, you can move back and forwards in it with the left and right arrow keys and make any needed changes before pressing RETURN.

Writer starts again. You see that *shred* has replaced the file with gibberish.

Close Writer, type *rm xyz123.odt* and press RETURN. The file is deleted.

Section 6.6 pointed out that, even when a file is deleted, it's still possible for an expert to recover its contents but anyone trying that with xyz123.odt would only recover the random gibberish.

You could have used shred -d xyz123.odt to overwrite the file and delete it in one step.

Of course, this time the file you destroyed was just a copy. LazyDog.odt is unaffected.

What you learned:

- **How to open the Terminal where you can type Linux commands.**
- **How to know which folder you're currently in.**
- **How to move to a different folder using the command line.**
- **How to use ping to check a network connection.**
- **How to use CTRL+C to force a program to quit.**
- **How to list the files in a folder using the command line.**

- How to copy a file using the command line.
- That you can start a graphical program such as Writer from the command line.
- How to use TAB to automatically complete a file name.
- How to modify and reuse commands you typed earlier.
- How to delete a file using the command line.
- How to use shred to delete a file so it can never be recovered.
- *Reasons to sometimes use the command line.*
- *That Windows has a similar command line.*
- *How to copy text from the Terminal window.*
- *That you can specify a file that isn't in the current folder.*

12.12 Root and sudo

This tells you how to become an omnipotent Unix God!

With Terminal open, type *ls -l ~* and press RETURN. A detailed list of the files and folders in your home folder appears.

Type man ls and press RETURN. Information appears about how to use the ls command. Press the down arrow key until you see the -l option: you see that it selects a long listing format.

You can type man (manual) followed by the name of any command line program to find out how to use it. Unfortunately the information is often extremely verbose and is rarely organised to make it easy to see how to do basic things.

Press q to get back to the prompt.

Each file or folder is listed on a separate line. At the left side, *d* indicates a directory (folder). The folder or file permissions follow (Section 12.9): the first three letters/dashes are for the owner, the next three are for the group and the last three for all other users. *r* indicates that a file can be read (viewed) and *w* shows it can be written to (changed) or deleted. *x* indicates it can be run as a program.

E.g. a file that shows -rwxr-x--- can be viewed, changed or run by its owner and viewed or run but not changed by other group members. Users who aren't group members can't view, change or run the file at all.

The file owner and group are shown: both of these should be your user name for most files in your home folder.

> *The file size in bytes and its modification date and time appear after the user and group. The file name itself is at the end of the line.*

Type *ls -l /etc* and press RETURN. You see details of the files in the *etc* folder. As mentioned in Section 6.1, files in this folder contain settings that affect the operating system itself.

You'll notice that most files in this folder belong to a user called **root**. Most of them can only be written to (changed by) root and some of them (e.g. *shadow* containing encrypted user passwords) can't be viewed by any other users (including you).

> *Files in other system-related folders such as bin, sbin, lib, usr and var are also mostly owned by root. Other users (or programs run by them) can't make changes that might damage the system. This arrangement keeps Linux systems well protected against viruses.*

So who is root and how can you as a mere mortal make changes when they really are needed?

> *Root is the super-user who can do anything on the system including viewing files belonging to all the other users.*

> *On most Linux systems, you can log in with the user name root. You normally need to enter a different password that you would have set when you installed the system. Ubuntu is different...*

With Ubuntu, you as an administrator can type *sudo* in front of a command. You'll be asked for your password, then the command runs as the root user.

> *As mentioned in Section 12.8, there can be problems starting Update Manager. Try typing sudo update-manager.*

> *You'll often see instructions to type something that starts with sudo. You must be very careful when you do this. You could damage or destroy your Ubuntu and Windows systems (though not the computer itself) or you could introduce malware.*

> *When you use a graphical tool such as Ubuntu Software Center or Users and Settings and it asks for your password, this is so that it can become root and make changes.*

Anyone attacking your system will strive to become root so they can steal files and passwords or install malware. They might try to trick you into doing something you shouldn't. This is known as **social engineering***.*

Except when you use it to log in, never type in your password unless you know why it's needed. If someone else tells you to, don't do it unless you really trust them.

Sometimes you'll find instructions to make changes to a configuration file using **vi** *(the infamous Unix command-line file editor). You can use the graphical gedit editor instead. E.g. type sudo gedit /etc/hosts instead of sudo vi /etc/hosts. Gedit is quite similar to Writer: it's much easier to understand than vi.*

Ordinary users such as the one you added in Section 12.9 can't use sudo: they can only mess up their own files. You can start Users and Groups and change the account type of another user to Administrator if you trust them to make system changes.

Type *exit* and press RETURN. Terminal closes.

What you learned:

- **How to see and interpret a detailed list of files.**
- **What the super-user (root) is.**
- **That most system files (the ones that aren't in users' home folders) are owned by the super-user and can't be changed by other users.**
- **How to become the super-user when you need to change something in one of these files.**
- **How to quit (exit) the terminal.**
- *How to use man to get information about a command.*
- *How permissions protect Ubuntu from malware.*
- *How to start Update Manager from the command line.*
- *What a Social Engineering attack is.*
- *To take care whenever you're asked for your password.*
- *How to use the gedit editor in place of the vile vi.*
- *How to allow other users to make system changes if you trust them.*

12.13 Checking your disk partitions

*Your hard disk can be divided up so it looks like more than one separate disk. These apparent disks are known as **partitions**.*

Section 3.7 mentioned that you can install Ubuntu on a separate partition instead of as a file within Windows (WUBI). It also mentioned converting a WUBI installation to one on a separate partition. Either of these lets Ubuntu run a bit faster and more reliably.

As you'll see here, the way that your disk is currently partitioned and used affects how easy it would be to do either of these things.

With Ubuntu running, click ▭ to start Nautilus. Click on any devices at the left side that aren't showing ⏏. As each one opens, it starts showing ⏏.

This indicates it's mounted (Section 6.4). Later on you'll check how much free space it has.

Click ⌕ File System on the left side, open the *host* folder, then right-click the *ubuntu* folder and click on *Properties*. The total size of files in the folder is shown. Make a note of it.

Click ⦿ and start Terminal. The command prompt appears. Type *sudo fdisk -l* into the terminal and press RETURN. You'll need to type your password, then you'll see something like this:

```
Device Boot Start      End      Blocks Id      System

/dev/sda1 *     2048    409599    203776 7 HPFS/NTFS/exFAT

/dev/sda2    409600  195722099 97656250 7 HPFS/NTFS/exFAT

/dev/sda3  195722100 233593715 18935808 7 HPFS/NTFS/exFAT
```

This shows that the hard disk currently has three partitions identified as */dev/sda1* to */dev/sda3*. The *System* type (*HPFS/NTFS/exFAT*) means that they're all used by Windows. The one with the largest number of blocks is normally the Windows *C:* drive. Make a note of its name (*/dev/sda2* in this case).

*Disks can have a maximum of four **primary** partitions but this often isn't enough. To get around the problem, an **extended** partition can be made in place of one of the four primary partitions. It can contain a number of further **logical** partitions.*

Linux usually numbers the primary partitions as /dev/sda1 to /dev/sda4. Logical partitions are numbered /dev/sda5 up. Some older computers may show hda instead of sda.

- If you only see one or two partitions or if you see one whose System says *Extended*, you wouldn't have any problems creating the two new partitions you'd need to move WUBI or to install Ubuntu from scratch from a DVD or thumbdrive. You might not have enough disk space though.

- If you see three partitions (as above), you'd need to create an extended partition too. That's only slightly more complicated.

- If you see four partitions and none is *Extended*, you'd need to delete one of the existing partitions before you can make an extended one. This often happens with Windows 7 computers. It's going to be a problem. The Ubuntu installer will only offer to make a WUBI installation (*Install Ubuntu inside Windows 7*), delete Windows and use the whole disk or let you set up the partitioning yourself. You'll need some expert advice.

*Instead of deleting a partition, you can buy or borrow a disk management utility such as **Partition Magic** that can convert it to a logical one.*

Type *df* and press RETURN. You'll see something like this:

Filesystem	1K-blocks	Used	Available	Use%	Mounted
udev	1336920	4	1336916	1%	/dev
tmpfs	537576	848	536728	1%	/run
none	5120	0	5120	0%	/run/loc
none	1343932	1336	1342596	1%	/run/shm
/dev/sda2	97656244	45988104	51668140	48%	/media/A
/dev/sda1	203772	29388	174384	15%	/media/S

You can see the amount of disk space used by the */dev/sda1* and */dev/sda2* partitions and how much is free (*Available*) on each one. Note that a 1K block is 1024 rather than 1000 bytes.

Normally, the partitions fill the disk and you'd need to shrink one or more of them to make room for new ones. The obvious candidate is the *Windows C:* partition (*/dev/sda2* in this case).

Shrinking a partition reduces the amount of free space on it. You can't shrink a partition to be less than its current used space.

In this example, /dev/sda3 isn't shown but the fdisk output shows that it's much smaller than /dev/sda2. There's not likely to be much point shrinking it.

To move WUBI, you'd need at least as much space in one of the new partitions as the *ubuntu* folder is using now. You can shrink the *Windows C:* partition so there's only a few megabytes free: once you're done you can remove WUBI (the *ubuntu* folder) leaving Windows with a reasonable amount of free space.

To install from scratch, you'd want at least 20-50 GB free for one of the new partitions.

In either case, the other partition (the swap one) would need 2-5 GB.

*Linux uses the **swap partition** to temporarily store data from the RAM if that gets full. It also uses it to save all RAM data when you hibernate the computer (Section 4.3). A larger swap partition means you can run more memory-hungry programs such as picture or video editors and you're less likely to have problems with hibernation.*

Now you can see if you've got enough disk space to do the move or installation.

- If you're short of space, you could consider backing up your documents, photos and music in WUBI (Section 6.7), then removing it (Section 12.14). That'll let you shrink the *Windows C:* partition more. You'd need to do a new installation from a DVD or thumbdrive, then restore your files. Alternatively, you could buy a bigger or additional disk but you might need help to install it.

- If you've got plenty of free space, consider how much you'll be using Ubuntu and how much you'll use Windows and choose the size for the Windows partition accordingly. If you'll mainly use Ubuntu, you'll want to shrink Windows almost as much as you can. If you'll still use Windows some of the time, you won't want to shrink it as much.

If you're installing Ubuntu from scratch and don't have four primary partitions, its installer can handle everything including shrinking the C: partition for you. Make sure you choose Install Ubuntu alongside the current operating system (Windows) or choose to set up the partitions yourself when asked. Your computer is unchanged until after you've done this: you can quit here if you get cold feet.

If you want to move your WUBI installation, don't have four primary partitions and have Windows Vista or 7, start it. Click ⊞, then click Control Panel on the right-hand side of the panel that appears. Type partition into the search box at the top right, then click on ⬤ Create and format hard disk partitions. The Disk Management program starts: you can right-click on the C: partition and choose Shrink Volume....

If you have Windows XP and want to move your WUBI installation, you'll need to use something like Partition Magic or use gparted with a live boot Ubuntu DVD.

You might decide that you don't want to mess with any of this and will just continue using WUBI. That's a sensible choice, especially if you already have four primary partitions, have limited free disk space or have Windows XP.

12.14 Removing WUBI

If you want to remove the WUBI version of Ubuntu (because you've moved it to a separate disk partition or you just don't like it), be sure to back up any important files first (Section 6.7). You can also copy them to Windows or to a new Ubuntu installation from WUBI itself.

Section 6.5 showed how the Windows drive C: can be accessed using Nautilus. Disk partitions belonging to any new Ubuntu installation show up in the same way and, permissions permitting (Section 12.9), you can copy files to any of them.

If you have Windows 7 or Vista, start it, click ⊞, then click *Control Panel* on the right-hand side of the panel that appears. Click 📋 Programs and Features in the window that appears. Scroll down the list of programs that appears until you see *Ubuntu*. Click on it so it's highlighted and click Uninstall/Change above the list. After a short delay, a new window appears. Click [Uninstall]. WUBI is removed.

If you have Windows XP, start it, click [🏁 start], then click *Control Panel* on the right-hand side of the panel that appears. Click or double-click 📋 (*Add or Remove Programs*) in the window that appears. Scroll down the list of programs that appears until you see *Ubuntu*. Click on it so it's highlighted and click *Change/Remove*. After a short delay, a new window appears. Click [Uninstall]. WUBI is removed.

If you decide that you prefer Windows to Ubuntu but want to continue using LibreOffice, a Windows version of it is available. The version of this book covering LibreOffice on Windows XP shows how to install it.

13 Mail merge

Mail merge is a word-processor feature that you can use to print personalised versions of a standard letter for people whose names and addresses are in a list somewhere on the computer. You'll have received many of these letters yourself.

Mail merge is an advanced feature but this book covers it since small businesses and organisations will often want to use it.

Before you do a mail-merge, you need to do some planning:

- Where are the names and addresses? Can you get them into Calc or export them as a file that Writer can use?

  You saw in Chapter 9 how tedious it is to type a lot of names and addresses. If the names and addresses are in a database, they can probably be exported as a CSV file, perhaps by the database administrator.

- Do you want to send the letter to everyone in the list? If not, is there information in the list itself that can be used to identify who should get a letter?

- Do you want to use windowed envelopes, sticky address labels or print the addresses directly onto envelopes?

  You can buy address labels and run them through the printer. Printing directly onto envelopes can involve a lot of trial and error. Windowed envelopes are easiest and the addresses and letters can't get out of step.

- Will you use pre-printed letterhead paper, a letterhead template or just plain paper?

- Do you have a scanned version of the signature you want to use?

  It's worth making one so you don't have to sign the letters individually by hand. Most scanners from well-known brands can be used with Ubuntu's Simple Scan program.

- What do you want the letter to say?

13.1 Making the address list

Start Nautilus by clicking ⬜ on the Launcher. Go to *Documents* and open *People.ods* (the spreadsheet you made in Chapter 9).

Click *File > Save As....* The *Save As...* dialogue box opens. Click ⬍ to the right of *All Formats* (above ⬚ Save ⬚) and click *Text CSV (.csv)* in the list.

> *You may need to move the mouse cursor over the triangle below the list to scroll down.*

Click ⬚ Save ⬚ . You may need to click ⬚ Use Text CSV Format ⬚ . Suitable field options are already set in the next dialogue box. Click ⬚ OK ⬚ . The address list is saved in *My Documents* as *People.csv*. Close the spreadsheet.

> *Almost all database programs can export CSV (**Comma-Separated-Values**) files although how to do that is outside the scope of this book. As you'll see later, you can get the addresses directly from the spreadsheet or from a LibreOffice Base database but now that the addresses are in a CSV file, you can use the same procedure wherever they came from.*

> *If you're interested, go to Documents, right-click on People.csv and click Open with Text Editor. The file opens in the gedit text editor program: it's as if the list was on paper tape and you'd printed it. Click ⊡ to make it easier to follow. You'll see how simple the file is. Data for the columns is separated with commas. The first line gives the column headings.*

> *If you have a CSV file from another source such as a database, you can start the procedure here. You should open the CSV file with gedit to see if it also separates the data with commas.*

What you learned:

- **How to export the addresses in the Calc spreadsheet as a CSV file.**
- *What a CSV (Comma-Separated-Values) file is.*
- *That addresses in other databases can be exported as a CSV file too.*
- *How to open a file with a program other than the one that saved it.*

- *How to view a simple text file using gedit.*

13.2 Making a template letter

Before you start this section, you need to make sure LibreOffice Base is installed. See Section 12.1.

Start a new Writer document or open your letterhead template.

Click *Tools > Mail Merge Wizard....* The **Mail Merge wizard** starts.

Select *Use the current document* and click | Next >> |.

Select *Letter* and click | Next >> |.

At the left of the Mail Merge Wizard dialogue box, you can see which step the wizard is at. It should now be at step 3. Insert address block.

Click | Select Address List... |. The *Select Address List* dialogue box opens. Click | Add... | and select the *People.csv* file.

You'll notice that you could choose the People.ods spreadsheet file instead of the CSV file.You can choose some other file types too including Excel spreadsheet and LibreOffice Base database files. When the data is in one of these forms, that's an easier way to use it but it wouldn't work with other databases.

Using a CSV file also lets you use your templates with different databases as described in Section 13.3.

Click | Open |. A *Text Connection Settings* dialogue box appears. Its settings should be OK if you're using *People.csv*. If you're using a file from a different source, you might need to make some changes, e.g. changing the *Field separator* from a comma to a semicolon or tab. Click | OK |.

LibreOffice converts the address list to a database which any LibreOffice document can use. It's added to the list in the *Select Address List* dialogue box and is highlighted. Click | OK |.

If you ever want to delete this database, click Tools > Options..., click ▶ next to LibreOffice Base and click on Databases. A list of registered databases appears. Click on People to select it, then click | Delete |.

Tick the tickbox next to *This document shall contain an address block.*

Click | More... |. Another dialogue box opens showing available formats for the address block. Click on the one that you want to use.

The address blocks use elements (fields) whose names are preset in LibreOffice. Their names seem to vary slightly from one installation to another and they probably don't match the fields in People.csv but we'll fix this in a bit.

If none of the address blocks are quite right, choose the best one and click | Edit... |. The Edit Address Block dialogue box opens where you can add or remove elements and rearrange them before clicking | OK |. You can use the two arrow buttons in the middle of the box to add or remove highlighted elements. Use the four arrow buttons at the right of the box to change the position of a highlighted element and add or remove spaces.

Click | OK | to close the *Select Address Block* box and click | Match Fields... |. The *Match Fields* dialogue box opens.

You see the address element names listed with a drop-down list next to each. Each one lists all the fields in *People.csv*. Look for elements that are actually used in the address block where the matching either says *<none>* or is incorrect. Choose the correct matches from the lists, then click | OK |.

The address block preview at the bottom also shows if there are problems: e.g. if <Address Line 1> isn't matched to the Address field in People.csv. You may need to scroll down to see some of the matchings.

Click | Next >> |. Make sure that the tickbox next to *This document should contain a salutation* is cleared.

The wizard doesn't handle salutations (Dear ...) well. It's easier to set the salutation up by hand later on.

Click | Next >> | twice and click | Edit Document... |. The wizard shrinks to a small box so you can work on the document. At the moment, it only contains the address block as a text frame (Chapter 11).

Click on the outline around the address block frame so that green square handles appear. If necessary, drag the frame until its top is about 5.5 cm (2.2 inches) from the top of the page and its left side lines up with the left margin. Drag the handle in the middle of the right side rightwards until the frame is about 7 cm (3 inches) wide.

These dimensions might not be right for the envelopes you'll use. You can measure the position of the window or measure the position of the address on an existing letter that fits correctly and use those measurements instead.

Click below the frame and press RETURN repeatedly until the text cursor is about 1 cm (0.4 inch) below the frame. Click *Insert > Fields > Date*. A date field is inserted showing today's date. Double-click on it. A dialogue box opens. Choose *Date* instead of *Date (fixed)* and choose the format you prefer, e.g. *Friday, December 31, 1999*. Click OK .

With Date (fixed), the date is set when you insert it and it won't change. This would be useful if you're writing a letter and keeping a copy on your computer. You'd want the date to always match that on the letter that you printed and sent off.

By choosing Date instead, the date when the letters are printed will appear.

Click below the date and press RETURN three times.

Type *Dear* and press SPACEBAR. Click *Insert > Fields > Other....* The *Fields* dialogue box opens. Click the *Database* tab and make sure *Mail merge fields* is highlighted under *Type*.

In *Database selection,* click ▶ next to *People*. You may need to do this again underneath.

You select the database (People) and click ▶ to see the tables it contains. Clicking ▶ next to a table shows the fields it contains. In this case, the table is also called People.

You see the field names from *People.csv*. Double-click *Title*. *<Title>* appears in the document after *Dear*. Click after it and press SPACEBAR. Double-click *Surname* in the dialogue box. *<Surname>* appears in the document.

You may need to drag the Fields dialogue box to see your document.

You can insert a field by double-clicking on it or by clicking to select it and clicking Insert .

Click Close to close the *Fields* box. Click below *Dear*, press , (comma), then press RETURN several times. Type *Yours sincerely* and press RETURN.

If you have a scanned signature, click *Insert > Picture > From file...*

and choose its file. Click on the inserted signature, anchor it to the blank line after *Yours sincerely* and drag its handles to make it the right size. You may want to type your name on another line below it.

If you don't have a scanned signature, put enough blank lines below *Yours sincerely* to make room for your signature, then type your name.

Ms Elise Gill

92 Gloddaeth St

BIRCHAM TOFTS

PE31 0OR

Wednesday, May 16, 2012

Dear <Title> <Surname>,

Yours sincerely

John Smith

If you click View > Field Names, details of the fields appear. You'll see that each field name includes the name of the address database and table you're using (People). Click View > Field Names again to hide the details.

Click 🖶. You'll be asked if you want to print a form letter. Click **No**.

The letter is printed as it appears on the screen, with one of the names and addresses. Check there's enough room for the signature. Fold the letter and try it in a windowed envelope (if you're planning to use them). Confirm that the address shows in the window and that the date line is comfortably below the window. If the address block doesn't line up, drag its frame a bit, then print and recheck the letter.

Click *Return to Mail Merge Wizard* (circled above). Click [Next >>] twice. Make sure that *Save starting document* is selected, then click [Save starting document]. Type a suitable name, e.g. *Form-Letter*. Click [⬍] above [Save], click *ODF Text Document Template (.ott)* in the list and click [Save]. Click [Finish] to close the wizard. Close Writer, discarding changes.

> *For a one-off letter, you can work through the wizard from start to end but it's handy to have a template with the signature set up and the address block and date in the right places.*

What you learned:

- **How to start the Mail Merge Wizard and have it create the address block for a new form letter.**
- **How to insert the date into your document and change its format.**
- **How to insert fields in the salutation line that import data from the address database.**
- **How to include your signature in the letter so you don't have to sign every copy.**
- **How to check and adjust the letter to fit a window envelope.**
- **How to save the form letter as a template.**
- *That the address list is imported as a LibreOffice Base database.*
- *That you can import addresses directly from a spreadsheet.*
- *That the database is registered in LibreOffice so that all documents can use it.*
- *How to delete a registered database.*
- *How to see details about fields that you've inserted into a document.*
- *That you can only use the templates with a specific database.*
- *That you can have an inserted date field stay fixed or have it update automatically.*

13.3 Preparing a form letter

Open the saved *FormLetter* template.

Click below *Dear* and type (pressing RETURN when you see ¶):

Now that you're years old, perhaps you're thinking about life insur-
ance.¶
¶
I can offer you a choice of excellent policies. Please give me a call.¶

Click before *years* and click *Insert > Fields > Other....* The *Fields*
dialogue box opens. Click the *Database* tab, then *Mail merge fields.*
Click ▶ next to *People* then, if necessary, ▶ next to *People* below. The
field names appear. Double-click *Age*, then click [Close].

Make sure there's a space before and after *<Age>* in the letter. Adjust
the rest of the letter so it looks nice.

Ms Elise Gill
92 Gloddaeth St
BIRCHAM TOFTS
PE31 0OR

Wednesday, May 16, 2012

Dear Ms Gill,

Now that you're <Age> years old, perhaps you're thinking about life insurance.

I can offer you a choice of excellent policies. Please give me a call.

Yours sincerely

John Smith

Click *Tools > Mail Merge Wizard....* The Mail Merge wizard starts.

LibreOffice automatically updates the database when changes
are made to the file that was used to create it. For example, if
you'd made the database directly from the People.ods
spreadsheet or from a LibreOffice Base database, changes to
addresses in the spreadsheet or database would automatically
appear in any form letters you send. However, since you made
the database from People.csv (which could have come from

anywhere), the People.csv file needs to be exported from the spreadsheet or database again to make sure that the addresses are up to date.

Click *3. Insert address block* on the left hand side of the dialogue box. Click | Select Different Address List... |.

Although you could select a different database here, the template's field names refer to People and it wouldn't work. You can trick LibreOffice into letting you use a completely different address list by also exporting it as People.csv. You'll need to make sure the field names are exactly the same as before (you can edit them with the gedit text editor, then click ▨).

We don't want to send the letter to everyone in the list. Click | Filter... |. The *Standard Filter* dialogue box opens. In its first row, choose *Age* from the *Field name* drop-down list, choose < from the *Condition* list and enter *65* in the *Value* box.

In the next row, choose *BMI* as the *Field name* and < as the condition and enter *30* in the *Value* box. Make sure the *Operator* box says *AND*.

This means that only people who are under 65 years old AND aren't overweight will get the letter.

*You can **filter** on text fields too. You can choose like as the comparison and use * in the Value box to represent any combination of letters, numbers, spaces, etc. E.g. Postcode like CF* OR Postcode like NP* would select anyone with a Cardiff OR Newport postcode.*

*You can use more than one * in the value. E.g. Surname like *t* selects people with a t anywhere in their surname (except the first letter because it's a capital).*

The filter affects all documents that use the same database for mail-merge. You can remove the filter by opening any of the documents and setting all the Field names in the Standard Filter dialogue box to - none -.

Click | OK |, then click | OK | to close the *Select Address List* box.

Click *7. Personalise document* on the left hand side of the *Mail Merge Wizard* dialogue box. Click | Edit individual document... |.

The document has the letter for each person on a separate page. There should be four of them: each shows the person's age. If you want, you can make changes to personalise them.

Click *File* > *Print....* The *Print* dialogue box opens. Click the *General* tab and check that the right printer is highlighted. Assuming that each letter is only a single page, click the *Page Layout* tab and set *Include:* to *Front sides / right pages*.

LibreOffice and OpenOffice have a long-standing bug causing them to print blank pages during a mail merge. Printing this way avoids the problem.

Click [Print]. The letters are printed.

Click *Return to Mail Merge Wizard.* Click [Next >>]. You can choose *Save starting document* and click [Save starting document] to save the master letter (e.g. as *Insurance*). You can also choose *Save merged document* to save the individual letters, either as multiple pages in a single document or as separate documents.

If you save the starting document (the master letter), you can use it again in the future, perhaps with a different filter.

Click [Finish] or [Cancel] to close the wizard. If you're using window envelopes, you can close Writer. Otherwise, click in the address frame, press CTRL+A to select all the fields and press CTRL+C to copy them to the clipboard. Continue with Section 13.4 to print envelopes or Section 13.5 to print labels.

Make sure that what you copy from the address frame are the fields with shaded backgrounds, not an address from an individualised letter.

What you learned:

- **How to make a new form letter using the template.**
- **That you can insert fields from the address database into the body of the letter itself.**
- **How to filter the recipients so only those meeting certain criteria get the letter.**
- **How to personalise and print the letters.**
- *That you shouldn't use the wizard to print – it inserts blank pages.*
- *That, if the database was created directly from a spreadsheet, it will stay up to date.*
- *That, if the database was created from a CSV file, the file should be updated.*
- *A way to use the template with a completely different address list.*
- *That you can use * to filter on just part of a text string.*
- *That you can set multiple filter rules and choose whether any or all must be met.*
- *That a filter is part of the database and will be used by other documents.*
- *How to remove the filter from the database.*

13.4 Printing envelopes

Follow this section if you want to print names and addresses onto envelopes.

With the form letter from Section 13.3 still open and the address block copied to the clipboard, click *Insert > Envelope...*. The *Envelope* dialogue box opens. Click the *Envelope* tab. Delete anything in the *Addressee* box. If you want a return address on the envelopes, tick *Sender* and type it into the box underneath.

Don't paste the address block into the Addressee box. Only one address would be pasted.

Click the *Format* tab and choose the envelope size. Click the *Printer* tab and choose how the envelopes will be loaded into the printer.

Click New Doc. . A new document is created for the envelopes. You'll see an empty text frame where the recipient's address should go. Click in it and press CTRL+V.

> *You can print an envelope for an ordinary letter in much the same way. If you click* Insert *instead of* New Doc. *, the envelope becomes the first page of the letter itself (you can print it separately by specifying a page range). In this case, you can paste or type the address into the Addressee box or into the empty text frame.*

Click *Tools > Mail Merge Wizard....* The wizard starts. Click step *7. Personalize document* and click Edit individual document... .

> *You see the individual envelopes. Check that they are showing different addresses. If they are all the same, you might not have copied the address frame fields correctly.*

Click *File > Print....* Again, click the *General* tab and check that the right printer is highlighted. Click the *Page Layout* tab and set *Include:* to *Front sides / Right pages*. You may need to load the envelopes into the printer before printing or feed them individually while printing. Click Print .

> *Take care to stack the letters and the envelopes in the order they are printed. This makes it much easier to match them up.*

Click *Return to Mail Merge Wizard.* Click Next >> . You can choose *Save starting document* and click Save starting document to save a template, e.g. *Envelopes*. You can use this to print envelopes for future letters.

Click Finish or Cancel to close the wizard. Close Writer once for the envelopes and again for the letter.

What you learned:

- **How to print envelopes for a form letter.**
- *How to print an envelope for an ordinary letter.*

13.5 Printing labels

Follow this section if you want to print names and addresses onto sticky labels.

With the form letter from Section 13.3 still open and the address block copied to the clipboard, click *File > New > Labels*. The *Labels* dialogue box opens. Click the *Labels* tab. Delete anything in the *Label text* box.

Lower down, select either *Continuous* (tractor fed labels, e.g. for a dot matrix printer) or *Sheet* (sheet fed labels – the commonest type). Select the *Brand* and *Type* of labels you'll be using.

LibreOffice knows the dimensions of many commercially available labels. When you select one of them, this information is set on the Format tab of the dialogue box.

If the labels you want to use aren't in the list or if the dimensions need adjusting, you can change them on the Format tab. If you do this, the label choice on the Labels tab automatically changes to [User].

Click the *Options* tab and make sure that the tickbox next to *Synchronize contents* is ticked.

Click New Document . A new document is made with a frame for each label on the sheet.

Click in the first (top left) frame and press CTRL+V. The address fields are pasted into the frame (they should have a grey background) and the text cursor should be after the last field (the postcode).

Click *Insert > Fields > Other....* A dialogue box opens. Click on *Next record* under *Type* and on *People* as the *Database*. Click Insert . Nothing visible happens. Click Close .

If you click View > Field Names, you'll see that a Next Record field has been inserted after the Postcode one. This tells LibreOffice to print the next recipient's details on the next label, even though it's on the same page.

Click in the first frame and press CTRL+A to select all the fields. Now you can change the font and/or click Format > Paragraph and change the spacing to make the address fit the label and look nice.

Click Synchronize Labels . The remaining labels on the sheet are filled in.

They may all be showing the same person. Don't worry.

Click *Tools > Mail Merge Wizard...*. The wizard starts. Click Step *7. Personalize document* and click | Edit individual document... |.

You see the labels ready to print. Click *File > Print...*. Again, click the *General* tab and check that the right printer is highlighted. Click the *Page Layout* tab and set *Include:* to *Front sides / Right pages*. Load the labels into the printer and click | Print |.

Take care to stack the letters and the sheets of labels in the order they are printed. This makes it much easier to match them up.

Click *Return to Mail Merge Wizard*. Click | Cancel | to close the wizard. Close Writer once for the labels and again for the letter.

What you learned:

- **How to print labels.**
- *That LibreOffice knows the dimensions for many available labels.*
- *That you can modify the dimensions for other labels or to fix glitches.*
- *How to change the font and line spacing for the addresses.*

14 Epilogue

I hope you've found this book to be clear, informative, useful and not too overwhelming or intimidating.

Next time you need to do something, you may remember that Ubuntu or LibreOffice can do it but not remember how. Check the index.

There are many features of Writer that the book hasn't covered. For example, you might want to format some paragraphs with a *drop capital* – a large letter at the start. LibreOffice Help shows how to do that.

There are many more features of the Calc spreadsheet and the Draw program left for you to discover.

Although web browsing is only covered very briefly and e-mail not at all, you'll have picked up enough conventions and jargon to have a good chance of figuring these out yourself.

There are many advanced topics not covered either. Linux is an incredibly powerful system. It can serve music and video files, power web sites (*Apache*), run databases, act as a telephone exchange (*Asterisk*) and far more beside – no expensive licenses required. It's also a great system if you want to write programs. Now you know the basics and some of the jargon, you might want to explore the possibilities.

Sometimes you'll think *Wouldn't it be useful if LibreOffice/Ubuntu could do such and such?* It probably can. Try the Help menu or a search engine.

Alphabetical Index

www.ingramcontent.com/pod-product-compliance
Lightning Source LLC
Chambersburg PA
CBHW051238050326
40689CB00007B/967